TRICKS WITH

YOUR HEAD

TRICKS WITH

YOUR HEAD

MAC
KING
AND
MARK
LEVY

ILLUSTRATED
BY BILL KING

THREE
RIVERS PRESS
NEW YORK

Published by Three Rivers Press, New York, New York.
Member of the Crown Publishing Group, a division of Random House, Inc.
www.randomhouse.com

THREE RIVERS PRESS and the tugboat design are registered trademarks
of Random House, Inc.

Printed in the United States of America

Design by Susan Maksuta

Library of Congress Cataloging-in-Publication Data

Levy, Mark, 1962–
    Tricks with your head / Mark Levy and Mac King; illustrated by Bill
    King.
        1. Magic tricks.   2. Head.   I. King, Mac.   II. Title.

    GV1559.L47 2002
    793.8—dc21   2001027983

    ISBN 0-609-80591-6
10 9 8 7 6

First Edition

CONTENTS

Why You Should Let Mac King Play Tricks with Your Head

PENN AND TELLER

Mac King, a coauthor of this treatise on how to make rude mischief and have people love you for it, is a god.

Why do we deify this man? After all, he's—let's not mince words—a hayseed. His taste in wardrobe is hand-me-down baggy. He says "Howdy!" a lot. And, most damning of all, he's a comedy magician.

And yet in Mac somehow all those embarrassing character traits are assets. When you see him on stage, he strolls out floppy-haired in an oversize plaid suit. The Las Vegas slot-machine-numbed moms and jaded fourteen-year-old females groan and look daggers at their dads and juniors who dragged them to see the damn corny magic show. Then something happens. They penetrate Mac's yokel pose and realize there's genius at work. Soon the air shrieks with their pinched-seagull-like laughter.

We use Mac's show as a test of new acquaintances. Not liking Mac is like not liking Carlsbad Caverns, or Lou Reed, or Krispy Kreme Donuts. It means there's something wrong with you.

Mac has an amazing mind. He invented, yes, invented the greatest impromptu dinner stunt in the modern world (Eyescream) and its sister (Zit Squeeze). This book contains a cosmos of such completely surreal, brilliant ideas: Dog Jaw, for example, will absolutely (and we know—we've tested it) make anybody scream laughing. How to Have the Air in Your Lungs Change Places with the Air in a Balloon is, well, just that, and actually works. A Singularly "Pourous" Head and Thumb Through Ear will make your little niece squeal. If you are mean and rotten and simply like to embarrass and hit others, Mac provides Smack! (we advise doing the latter only on people smaller than you). And if you just want to have people laugh at and not with you, try Rubber Cement Retard.

Mac King has written jokes, tricks, and gags for us. And now he's doing the same for you. They could give you a career, or make you the life of the party or get you a black eye—or, more likely, all three. A god has smiled upon you. Count your blessings.

Mark Levy, Super Genius

MAC KING

Many, many years ago I had an idea. I thought it would be fun to write a book about tricks you could do using your head. I made some notes, wrote up a few of the tricks, and got my cousin Bill to do a few drawings in exchange for a forty-ounce bottle of malt liquor. That's really as far as I went with my little notion. Everybody thought it was cool, but I didn't have the time, or the assertiveness, to push it from vision to fulfillment. But then I met Mark Levy.

I was familiar with Mark because I knew he was the magic adviser on *Magic for Dummies* (by far the best introduction to conjuring available to the general public). He came by my house one afternoon to talk about some Las Vegas writing project he was working on, and I conned him into taking a look at the preliminary chapters of my book. He got excited. He didn't have the time to work on it either, but he certainly had the assertiveness. The book you have in your hands would not exist without Mark taking a huge chunk of his nonexistent time to write at least half of the tricks, and busting his assertive butt to go out and sell it to the publisher.

That he's a fine human being and a great magician you'll have to take my word on. That he's a creative genius, a startlingly wonderful writer, and a remarkably influential pitchman, you can prove to yourself by reading this book.

TRICKS WITH YOUR HEAD

THE HEADLESS WONDER

"IF YOU CAN KEEP YOUR HEAD
WHEN ALL ABOUT YOU ARE LOSING THEIRS . . .
YOU'LL BE A MAN, MY SON!"
—RUDYARD KIPLING

While Kipling's poetic counsel may have inspired many a lad to a life of noble achievement, such austere advice is deadly at a party. Rather than keeping your head, which anyone can do, you should lose it—and hear the laughter begin!

What They See: Over dinner, your companion gradually becomes aware that she is doing all the talking. Slowly

it dawns on her that the reason for this is that you have no head.

What Actually Happens: Half the preparation for this trick takes place at home, while you're dressing for dinner; the other half takes place at the performance site.

First, your home preparation: For "The Headless Wonder" to work, you must be wearing a button-front shirt and a pair of pants (or a skirt). Also, you must not wear an undershirt of any kind. Otherwise, your clothing choices are optional and will probably be dictated by peer pressure.

Second, your performance site preparation: You'll need a few minutes alone, so wait until your audience has to leave the table (to go to the bathroom, for example). To hasten her departure, throw a glass of red wine on her. If you're out with a group, try a pitcher of daiquiris. (Do we have to think of everything for you readers?)

However it happened, you are now alone. At this point, unbutton the top two or three buttons of your shirt, move your collar back behind your neck, and rebutton your collar button.

Still seated, duck your head under the table. (This is not as easy as it sounds, particularly if you're a bit heavy. Quickly lose twenty pounds and continue.) While in this position, use your hands to feel around above the tabletop, and make certain your collar is flush up against the table's edge. Also make sure that your collar is still roughly circle-shaped, as if your neck were still in it.

Complete the illusion by picking up your fork in one

hand and your knife in the other and holding them in the ready-to-eat position above the table. Periodically scratch inside the open neck hole with the tines of your fork as you wait for your wine- or daiquiri-soaked companion(s) to return to the table. You'll know they've returned when you hear them scream.

Notes: A bonus tip for the brave (or stupid): Instead of scratching your neck hole with a fork, try pouring your drink into it.

We instructed you to leave off your undershirt so that when your audience looks at your headless torso they see skin, not cotton. On the other hand, you're not trying to fool anyone with this gag. Think of it as bringing them joy, in the same way visiting dogs bring joy to nursing home residents, or collisions delight the crowds at funny-car rallies.

CAT CHIROPRACTOR

What They See: You're visiting your friend's parents. They have a cat. You ask them the following questions: "Is your cat fussy? Does he sleep away most of the day? When he is awake, does he make a meowing noise?" They of course

answer in the affirmative. "Aha! He needs a chiropractic neck adjustment!" you exclaim. As you pick up the poor beast and twist his head, an alarming "Crraaaack!" issues forth from his unfortunate vertebrae as you perform your feline alignment. You place the cat back down and he walks away. Of course he's still fussy, sleepy, and noisy, but at least

now he's comfortable. Please read the how-to part of this item before you try it. There is a trick to it. Don't actually twist a cat's head until his neck snaps. Unless it's your cat; then we believe you should be allowed to do whatever you want with it.

What Actually Happens: Obviously (at least to most people) it's not the cat's neck that cracks, so you need something to simulate that sound. Here are the four best things. . . .

The finest item for this is a plastic cup. Not just any plastic cup, though. You need the kind that is the most "clear." Perhaps it's better to say "the least cloudy." Anyway, when you crush one of these, it really shatters—making an uncommonly ghoulish imitation of splintering bones. Clandestinely deposit one of these cups in your armpit. Make sure that the cup is not directly touching your skin because when the cup shatters its edges can be sharp. Proper chiropractic care does not involve blood. Also, it helps if you're wearing a jacket to further conceal the cup, but this is not essential; trust us, everyone is diverted by the wild-eyed look of the poor cat as you grip its little head. Don't actually twist the cat's head. Once again, DO NOT actually twist the cat's head. Hold the cat in your right arm, and lightly grip its little head in your left palm like a softball; turn your left hand and arm like you're twisting open the lid on a big jar of pickles. Your left hand and arm turn, but the cat's head stays motionless. As you are pretending to ratchet the cat's head around, clamp down firmly with your arm on the unseen cup to produce the heart-stopping, bone-on-bone crunch. Set the cat down and give a benevolent smile to its horrified owner.

The next best thing for this is an empty plastic water bottle, sans lid. Just place this under your arm, and follow the instructions for the preceding cup version.

It's also possible to use a plastic Tic-Tac box. Just hold it in your right hand (that's the one with a cat in it), and crush the little box at the appropriate time. Another alternative is to covertly deposit a piece of dried macaroni in your mouth and bite down on it as you revolve the cat's head. This last one is kind of weak and not really recommended. Actually, the last two versions are pretty lame, and we only include them because one day you may have a cat trick emergency and they could save your keester. Like, for instance, say David Letterman was at your door and was going to put you on TV if you had a Stupid Pet Trick. If you were running around your house and couldn't find a plastic cup or a water bottle, but you did find a single crusty piece of dry macaroni at the back of the silverware drawer, you'd thank us then, boy.

BOOMERANG GUM

While watching a prominent TV show, the revered magician Paul Harris saw a wispy schoolgirl perform the following trick. The interesting thing about the girl's performance? She apparently convinced the audience that

this was "the real thing"—a genuine display of skill—rather than a trick. The moral for you, reader? Don't pooh-pooh the effects in this book without first attempting them on national television. Or, put another way: The next time you turn up your nose, you'd better produce a drinking straw from it (p. 69).

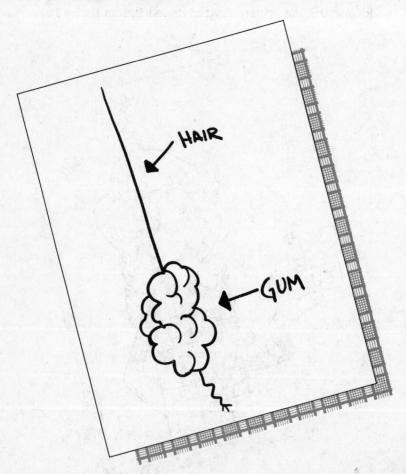

What They See: You spit out a wad of chewing gum, which circles back, impossibly, into your mouth.

What Actually Happens: We need to admit that neither of us has ever performed this trick. Not even Paul Harris has tested it. The reason? None of ours is long enough. . . . We're talking, of course, about our hair.

For this trick to work, you need to have a head full of long hair. How long? We suspect that hair which hangs down, at least, to the bottom of your chin is the minimum length required to do this effect.

Okay, then. To prepare, separate a single strand of hair from its neighbors, while keeping this lonesome hair attached to your head. The hair you choose should be from the very middle of the front of your head o' hair (directly above your mouth). Now chew gum.

After a minute of serious mastication, remove the gum and encircle it around the tip of your chosen hair strand. Make sure the gum wad is right at mouth level on the strand of hair. Congratulations, you now have a pendulum growing out of the front your head (see p. 24).

Familiarize yourself with the gum-on-hair's movements. Bow your head forward. Lean back. Lean your noggin from side to side. Work out a scheme of movements that make the gum's movements circular. When you've got that down, gently house the gum in your mouth, open, and start the circular motion from there. Practice until it genuinely looks like you're spitting the gum out, only to have it fly back. Some advice: Don't show off. Don't jerk the gum around in a million fancy directions before it zips back into your mouth. Gum pyrotechnics are sure to tip the method. K.I.C.S.—Keep It Circular, Stupid.

To perform, have the gum-on-hair combo already strung together in your mouth. Say something witty, like "Watch this!" Spit out the gum, let it fly, and suck it back into your mouth. Continue chewing. Perhaps you'll be able to break the tip of the hair off of the gum. If not, go to the bathroom and either snip the hair, or bite it off. Toss the gum, unless you like its new, hairy flavor.

Notes: For this trick, light-colored hair works better than dark hair, because the lighter shade is harder to detect against your skin. If you have dark hair, you'll want your spectators to stand farther away from you, so they don't pick up flashes of the clandestine hair. Paul Harris, of course, doesn't know for certain how the schoolgirl accomplished her stunt. But he'd bet his sponge balls that she used this gum-on-hair method, too. . . . The best people to perform this trick? Male rock stars and women.

FUNNEL IN PANTS

What They See: Explaining that this is the latest party craze at exclusive Hollywood gatherings, you propose a friendly game of skill. Give your friend a quarter and a funnel. Tell him to stick the narrow end of the funnel down the front of

his pants. Then have him tilt his head back and place the quarter flat on his forehead. Inform him that the idea is for him to straighten his head up, allowing the quarter to fall forward and to attempt to catch the coin in the funnel. Make it clear that he is not allowed to use his hands. As soon as he leans back and reaches up to place the quarter on his head, you pick up a glass of water and quickly dump it into the funnel. Man, this is funny.

What Actually Happens: No real explanation is necessary. Get a funnel. Get a quarter. Get a glass of water. Get a friend that you don't need anymore. The soon-to-be former friend should not have any idea that the water has anything to do with the little "innocent" game they're going to play. Appeal to your victim's competitive nature. Mention that Jerry Seinfeld can do this nine out of ten times. We repeat: This is funny.

If someone tries this on you, act as innocent as possible, but pretend to not understand what the trickster is asking you to do. Get the person to demonstrate, and turn the tables on him. But don't even bother pouring the water into the funnel; just pick up the glass and toss the water on his chest. That'll show 'em.

TELEKINETIC TIP

Telekinesis is the supposed production of motion in a body without the application of material force. TV star Drew Carey is a fan of strippers. How can those two sentences possibly be related? Well, one night many years ago (it was

so many years ago that Drew Carey was opening for Mac), Drew talked Mac into visiting a strip club with him and their buddy Al Canal.

For those of you who've never visited one of these places, it's only important to know that if you're sitting ringside when a young lady dances over near you, it's appropriate to give her money. The general method for proffering this tip is to tuck it into one of her remaining pieces of clothing. Mac knows this because when he was in college, he worked for a while at a lovely club in Louisville called the Merry-Go-Round. But it turns out that at the place Drew had taken him, protocol called for the patron to set the money down on the edge of the stage in order for the dancer to come over to retrieve it. It was sort of like bait.

What They See: On the particular night in question, Mac folded a dollar bill pup-tent style and placed it down at the stage's edge. As the lovely woman swirled her way over to our heroes, the dollar began to slowly creep toward her of its own volition. The woman let out a little twitter, but her nervousness at the haunted currency didn't prevent her from picking up the dollar using her own remarkable little trick.

What Actually Happens: To make a dollar bill move, first fold it in half lengthwise. Rest it in front of you on the table so that it forms a tiny tent. The big secret is—your breath. That's right, you merely blow on it. Because the secret is so incredibly simple, you have to direct attention away from that rudimentary solution. You do this by waving your fingers, hands, and arms at the money as if you are trying to push it away from you without touching it. Practice this a few times before you try it in public and you'll quickly see how much breath you need, and at what angle you need to blow. Don't pucker your lips up like a flute player, and don't make any noise; you are SECRETLY blowing on the bill.

If you're under age, or just don't particularly care for strip clubs, you can do this at the counter in a fast-food restaurant.

As for the trick the young lady used to pick up Mac's dollar that night? Well, that's the subject of a different book.

BITING OFF A PIECE

What They See: As you are taking a refreshing sip of your ice-cold pink circus lemonade, you accidentally bite down on the edge of the glass and a loud "snap" is heard as a shard of glass is broken off in your mouth. You spit this

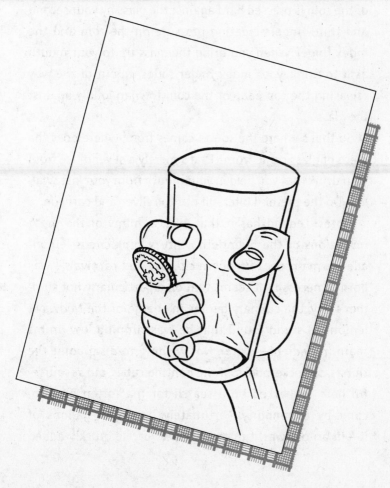

piece of glass back into your drink and carry on as if nothing were wrong.

What Actually Happens: To bite off and spit out a piece of a drinking glass you need to conceal a quarter (or a half-dollar is even better) in the fingers of your right hand as it is holding a glass. The top third of the coin is clipped between your right first and second fingers. The remainder of the coin is pressed hard against the glass by your second and third fingers creating pressure on the coin and the index finger. When you bring the glass up to your mouth as if to drink, your index finger slides up out of the way releasing the top edge of the coin to snap loudly against the glass.

So that's where the sound comes from; where does the piece of glass come from? That's merely a sliver of ice from your drink that you held in your mouth from your last swallow. Do the pretend bite, spit out the sliver, and carry on.

Notes: Legend has it that, like so many of the great inventions of the twentieth century, pink circus lemonade—a mainstay of modern circuses and carnivals—was born of necessity. It seems that on a particularly hot summer's day, the culinary genius in charge of the Midway's lemonade stand found that he was running low on his main ingredient—water. Not wishing to disappoint the thirsts, or pocketbooks, of the panting rubes, our resourceful hero embarked on a search for that often hard-to-come-by commodity. Fortunately he found gallons of it—in an old washtub on the back lot. He quickly added sugar and lemons, and in no time at all was filling cups with the festive nectar.

However, a strange phenomenon had taken place. It turns out that the water had just been used by an acrobat to clean his bright red tights, thus giving the lemonade its pink hue. Mmm-mmmm—pink circus lemonade.

Next Week: The origins of brown sugar.

Once upon a time, Mac was sitting at a restaurant eating a big hunk o' beef (because that's what you eat when visiting Argentina; they've got some good beef) when all of a sudden Mac's friend Max Maven exclaimed to him, "I have the perfect head trick for you!"

Mac said, "You should do it for the group." They were sitting with about ten of the finest magicians in Buenos Aires.

"No," Max replied, "it's too stupid for me to do. But it would be perfect for you." Being Max Maven, the most mysterious mind reader in the world, he had a reputation to uphold.

"Alrighty, show me how," Mac said, "and I'll do it for them." By now they had attracted the attention of the group. Mac borrowed a deck of cards from Alba, one of the Argentine magicians, and followed Max into another room of the restaurant. All the magicians thought they were going off to discuss some hush-hush, high-level, top-secret, backroom mystery. They were very excited when Mac told them he would perform the trick for them upon their return. Max was right; the trick was good. And so easy that with only one run-through Mac was ready to dazzle the South Americans with it.

What They See: Mac spread the cards out facedown on

the table. He had Alba pick a card from any part of the deck. Then she showed her card to the other folks so that they felt involved in the process. She returned the card anywhere she wanted to the still-spread deck. Then she gathered up the cards and squared up the deck before handing it back to Mac. "Fair enough?" Mac asked. All the magicians agreed that, indeed, it was very fair. Finding the card would be tough.

Mac asked Alba to extend her hand. He held it close to his face and took a big sniff. "Ah, now I have your scent. It should be easy to find your card." He began to fan through the cards, smelling them as he slowly passed them a few at a time under his bloodhound-sensitive nose. At one point he took a bigger whiff and one card rose up out of the fanned pack, stuck to his nose. Then as it cleared the top edge of the deck, the card did a forward flip, ending up face-outward in Mac's mouth. It was Alba's card!

What Actually Happens: Get yourself a deck of cards and a purdy smellin' woman and you're set! The first step to doing this is to know what card has been selected. This requires a tiny bit of preparation, but it's worth it. As all the magic-trick catalogues say, "This will fool the wise ones!" Secretly arrange the deck in order, ace through king of clubs, ace through king of hearts, ace through king of spades, and ace through king of diamonds. Bring out the deck, spread it facedown before your pretty woman (if no pretty woman is available, improvise).

Have her slide out a card from the spread and show it around. This is important. The people have to know what the card is, or the ending is stupid. Have her return her card back to the deck anywhere she wants, and then gather up the cards. Ask her to hold out her hand. Give it a good sniffing.

Now, because of the prearranged pack you'll be able to tell which card is hers. It's the only card not in the right order! Hold the cards up to your face and transfer them one or two at a time from your left hand to your right. You're holding the cards in your left hand with the faces toward you and pushing the cards off the face of the pack with your left thumb and receiving them in your right hand. Make sure no one but you can see the faces of the cards.

When you come to the selected card (remember, it's the one out of order) slightly lower your head so that your nose touches the center of the face of the selection.

Press the deck to your nose, and then slowly tilt your head up, increasing the volume of your sniff, and gradually drag the selected card up out of the fan with your nose (see figure 1). As the lower edge of the card clears the rest of the fanned-out deck, the top edge of the selected card will begin to tilt out toward the audience. At the same time, the bottom edge of the selection will automatically come in contact with your lips. Grasp the lower edge of the tilting card between your lips and let the card continue its flip away from you, so that its face is revealed to the audience

(see figure 2). If you remembered to have everybody look at the card when it was selected, then they should be impressed at this point. Trust us, not only does this really work, it's really easy.

A ROLL OF QUARTERS

What They See: Challenge your little sister to a game. Place a blank sheet of paper on the table in front of her. Give her a quarter and tell her to hold it between the tips of her two thumbs, so that the quarter is like a little wheel,

and her thumbs are like the axle going through the middle of the wheel. Now have her hold the quarter so its edge rests at the top of the bridge of her nose. Ask her to lean over the table so that the tip of her nose is positioned about six inches directly above the center of the piece of paper.

Now have her roll the quarter down her nose like a tiny wheel. Tell her when it reaches the tip of her nose to let go of the quarter and allow it to drop on to the paper. Assuming the quarter comes to rest on the paper, you reach over and draw a circle around the quarter where it lies. Have her pick up the quarter and perform the same set of rolling-down-her-nose-and-dropping actions that she did before. Tell her that the object of this little game is for her to get the quarter to rest more than halfway inside one of the ever-increasing-in-number pencil circles. If she does this in less than fifteen tries, she can keep the quarter.

Each time she rolls the quarter down her nose and drops it onto the paper, you draw another quarter-sized circle around it. Thus, every time she drops the quarter, there are more circles for her to land in, and her odds of winning continue to improve.

What Actually Happens: What you don't tell her is that every time you draw a circle around the quarter, the rough edge of the quarter is being coated with pencil lead. Pencil lead that is then transferred directly to her nose by her rolling actions. Of course it is possible for her to win this game, but you don't care. It is certainly worth twenty-five cents to see all the pencil marks the rolling quarter has left on her nose.

SPAGHETTI-EATING CONTEST

Any time Mac does a show for kids he does this trick. His pal David Williamson, who also does it in all his shows for kids, first showed it to him. You don't have to have an actual show to do this; just grab a couple of kids. Be careful how you go about this kid acquiring; the kidnapping laws are getting more and more strict.

What They See: You challenge a few kids to a spaghetti-eating contest. It looks like you're going to lose, but at the last minute you pull out the victory in an amazingly hilarious manner.

Line the kids up and tell them you're going to have a spaghetti-eating contest. Take a spool of thread and break off a piece for each kid. Each kid's piece o' thread should be long enough to hang from her mouth to about six inches above the floor. Take a piece of thread for yourself, too.

Instruct everybody to put one end of the thread in his or her mouth, allowing the rest of the thread to hang down toward the floor. You do the same. Tell them to put their hands behind their back. Again you follow suit. Explain that the thread represents spaghetti, and the first one to get her entire piece of spaghetti into her mouth without using her hands is the winner.

"On your mark, get set, go!" you announce. Everyone commences to chewing, tongue-twirling, and lip-puckering, trying with all their might to be the first to get their thread safely ensconced in their oral cavity. Everyone, that is, except you. You watch the others calmly. Just as one of the hapless participants is about to win, you suddenly zip the entire thread up into your mouth in one unexpected slurp. You win!

What Actually Happens: While it looks as if you have some sort of mechanical thread-reeling-in device hidden in your mouth, you do not. When you're ready to zip the thread up into your mouth, lean your head down so that your mouth is directly over the dangling thread. The thread should be hanging there in space, not touching your chest or chin. Form the opening of your mouth into a tiny, puckered "O" shape (sort of the shape you'd form if you were going to actually slurp in a real piece of spaghetti).

Now, suck in hard and steady through your pursed lips. The idea is to create a thin column of air surrounding the thread and moving quickly into your mouth. This airflow draws the lightweight thread right along with it into your mouth. Using this technique you can suck in a five- or six-foot length of thread in the blink of an eye. It almost appears as though the thread disappears, it gets sucked in so powerfully fast.

Notes: Exercise a bit of caution; you don't want to suck the thread up into your nasal cavity or down into your epiglottis. And, you don't have to do this with kids; the right adults will get a kick out of it, too.

THUMB THROUGH EAR

This trick is a variation of a stunt commonly known among Japanese schoolchildren. We caution you, then, to refrain from performing it if you peer out into your audience, and notice a sea of Japanese schoolchildren staring back at you. If you do perform the stunt under that circumstance, your audience reaction is likely to be "So?" (or its Japanese-language equivalent).

What They See: While scratching your ear, your thumb accidentally penetrates the ear-y flesh, and gets stuck. After a brief struggle, you free the thumb, leaving your ear no worse for the wear.

What Actually Happens: Here's an overview of the method: Using one hand, you're going to wrap the top and bottom part of your ear around your thumb (like a roll around a hot dog), and hold the setup in place with your index finger.

Here's the method in detail: Bring your open right hand up to your right ear, and turn the hand over, so your thumb is your finger closest to the floor.

Clip the top third of your ear deep within the space between your thumb and index finger, and lever your hand down 180 degrees, so your open palm is now touching the side of your face, and your knuckles face out to the right.

Use the tip of your right index finger to grab your ear-lobe, and gently pull the lobe into your fist. If you look in a

mirror, you'll probably surprise yourself with the considerable realism of the illusion: It looks like your thumb is jutting through the middle of your ear.

To further the illusion, lightly tug the ear up and down, back and forth, as if you've snagged the finger in your flesh, and you're trying your damnedest to extricate it. Ha! Now you're a magician (or a Japanese school kid)!

To perform, pretend that your ear itches. Scratch it vigorously, turning that side of your head away from the audi-

ence in the process. Quickly clip your ear, flip it, and give a painful little cry of "Jeez! I think I somehow got stuck my finger through my ear. Does it look bad?" Turn toward your audience, while you give the setup soft tugs.

They'll be expecting some harmless little prank, and will, instead, see a rather convincing, gruesome situation. Sometimes, a squeamish spectator will run away (true!).

To "free" your thumb, grimace, as you pull your hand backward with apparent difficulty. Turn away from the audience, and "wrench" your hand from its fleshy trap.

Notes: Hiro Sakai, a prominent Japanese magician (who used to be a Japanese school kid), came up with this one-handed version of a stunt that's normally performed with two hands.

TOO MANY PIPS

What They See: Snatch the orange slice from your date's drink. Bite out the juicy fruity part. Say, "Uhhh. A seed." Spit out a seed. Say, "Ouch, another one." Spit out another seed. Say, "Dang, there's another one." Spit out another one. Say, "There sure do seem to be a lot of seeds in that one thin orange slice," as you spit out about twenty more seeds in quick succession.

What Actually Happens: To do this you need to save about twenty-five or thirty orange seeds. Or, if you're not that anal-retentive, you can buy a bag of dried white beans. When no one is paying attention to you (which you could be noticing is happening more frequently if you've been trying out an unusually large number of the grosser stunts in this book), secrete a small handful of the seeds in your mouth. To regain attention, snatch that orange slice out of your pal's drink. If your date isn't drinking something containing an orange slice, either date someone else (who wants to invest in a relationship with someone who might die any second from scurvy), or simply order a Shirley Temple your own self. Follow the scenario in the last paragraph.

As with most of the feats in this book, it is best to practice this a few times in private before attempting it in public. There is a bit of an inside-the-mouth management knack necessary to coordinate the seeds and the bitten off piece of fruit. You want to be able to swallow the fruit but not the seeds, and then to be able to spit out the seeds singly (they tend to get clumped together by your saliva and the orange juice).

This feat was donated by Tom Mullica, who used it for years in his terrific magic act at The Crazy Horse in Paris.

USING YOUR HEAD TO BEAT A SPEEDING TICKET

What They See: Let's say you've committed some minor traffic violation and have been pulled over by the police. This is the trick for you. First, get out of the car. Police officers love that. Right off the bat you've endeared yourself. Next, ask if he'd like to see a magic trick. Don't wait for his response; just immediately grab his ticket book and pen from his hand. Say, "I'll tap this book with the pen three times, and on the third tap the book will disappear." Instead, on the third tap the pen disappears.

The vanish is exposed by showing that you left the pen behind your ear on the final tapping motion. By now the officer is no doubt intrigued, and well on his way to being your buddy. Removing the pen from behind your ear and once again tapping his book, this time you succeed in making his book disappear. With a merry wave and a hearty, "Good day sir," you get back in your car and motor away. Once again, magic has saved the day.

What Actually Happens: Before we get to the explanation, let's just clarify something. You shouldn't really do this with a police officer. At least, we don't think you should. If you actually try this with an officer of the law and live to tell about it, please let us know how it goes.

All right, on to the how-it's-done part: You need to be wearing a jacket with side pockets. If those pockets have flaps, tuck them in. You also need a pen and a small pad of paper that will fit into one of those jacket pockets.

When you're ready to show someone this trick, face her directly and then turn slightly to your right. Show the pad in your palm up left hand. Hold the pen in your right hand as if it were a dart you were about to throw. Announce that you will tap the pad three times, and that on the third tap the pad will disappear.

Raise the pen up even with your right ear. Bring the pen down and tap the pad, saying, "One." Repeat the actions, counting, "Two." Again raise the pen to your right ear in preparation for the count of three. On the way up, without hesitation, your right hand slides the pen behind your ear and leaves it there. Swing your right hand down to the pad, counting, "Three." The third tap should look no different than the first two. The effect you are striving for is that instead of the pad vanishing on the third tap, the pen disappeared.

After the vanish of the pen has registered, pull back both your elbows, thus bringing your hands closer to the tops of your jacket pockets. It should look as if you're searching for the lost pen. Continuing to look for the pen, you now turn to your left. Because of this slight turn to the left, your body now blocks your left hand (and the pad) from view. It is a simple matter to secretly deposit the pad of paper into your left jacket pocket. This is amply covered by suddenly "noticing" the pen behind your ear, thus directing attention up and away from your hands.

With your right hand, reach up and remove the pen from your ear, and hold it as before. Keep your left hand cupped a bit, as if still holding the pad. "Let's start again at three," you say as you turn back to face the spectator. Tap your cupped left hand with the pen, counting, "Three." When tapped, your left hand opens out flat to show that the pad is gone. The impression you're trying to convey is that the pad vanished at the very instant you tapped it.

That's it. Except for one other thing. We were kidding, you should definitely do this for the police.

What They See: You corner a friend, and announce, "You have a big brain, a very, very big, heavy brain. In fact, if you had no arms or legs, your torso wouldn't even be strong enough to lift that fat, powerful brain you have swimming

around inside your head." Offering to prove your claim, you ask your friend to take several paces back from a wall, and lean forward, until the top of his head rests against the wall. Now, without moving his arms or feet, you dare him to pick his head up, using torso power alone. He can't do it—proving his intellectual superiority.

What Actually Happens: Physiological mechanics. When you have your friend stand in a certain position, his body can't generate the balance it needs to stand.

Here's the tricky position: Have him butt his face up against a wall, and then take three steps backward, away from the wall. Now have him lean all the way forward, until his hands stop him (with a smack!). Ask him to rest the top of his head against the wall, and let his hands dangle down at his sides. He physiologically can't budge from this position, as long as he keeps his legs and arms motionless.

Applaud the heft of his brain, as you carefully scarf his wallet from a back pocket.

Notes: It will be easier to talk your friend through this if you've actually tried it yourself, so that you thoroughly understand the position your body needs to be in relative to the wall.

ZIT SQUEEZE

First, this is a great trick. Second, it's really gross. Third, as you've probably gathered, in our minds great and gross are strongly connected.

What They See: "Man, is this zit bothering me. It's the kind that hurts; you know what I mean?" You continue as if this were the perfect conversational tidbit to be tossing out when you're having dinner for the first time with your girlfriend's parents. "It's one of those with the hard little ball of something trapped just under your skin that just won't come out no matter how hard you squeeze. The kind that, when you stop squeezing, sends a sharp pain straight up to your brain. Usually I only get that kind on the inside of my ear, but I've got this one right here in the middle of my face. Is it noticeable at all? 'Cause it feels like a daggone boulder is perched on my cheek."

If old M & P are still seated with you, reach up and squeeze the offending oil-boil. It bursts, and a thin strand of dirty yellow suppuration oozes forth from your face. And by "suppuration," we mean nasty, pus-colored, viscous, ulcerated chancre matter. It comes out in one solid foot-long, vermicelli-sized tassel of zit discharge. Pure poetry.

What Actually Happens: All you need is a packet of very soft butter and either a toothpick or a fork to poke a hole in the wrapper of the butter. There are two types of wrapped butter packs that work for this stunt: the packs that are a very thin plastic dish topped with a foil peel-back cover, and the packs where the pats of butter are wrapped up like tiny Christmas presents. Either kind will be perfect.

With one tine of the fork (or the toothpick) poke a small hole in your butter pack. If it's the two-piece, plastic/foil combo container, poke the hole in the center of the foil lid.

If you're dealing with the one that's just wrapped in foil, poke the hole in the center of the top of the package; that's the surface you'd put the bow on if it really were a tiny Christmas present. This little poke happens below the tabletop away from the prying eyes of your future in-laws

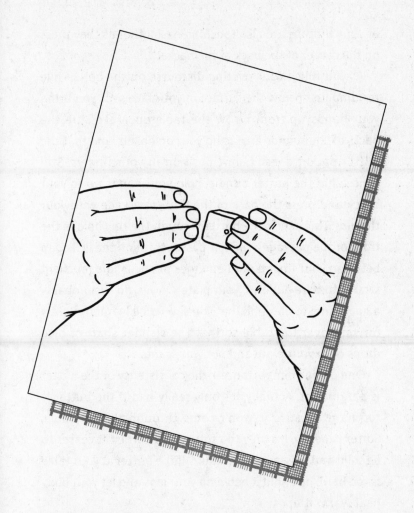

(whatever else you do below the tabletop, out of their view, is of no concern to us). Touch the four fingertips of your left hand to the four fingertips of your right hand with the packet positioned so that its hole corresponds to the little window between your second and third fingertips. The tips of your thumbs are also touching each other as they press on the center of the back of the packet.

As you finish your riveting discourse on the boil of bile residing just below the surface of your face skin, you bring your hands up from below the tabletop. Make sure the backs of your hands are facing your onlookers, and that the butter packet doesn't shift position in your fingers. Still concealing the butter bundle, hold your hands up to your cheek and press the back of the butter package with your thumbs. This expels the butter through the tiny hole in the front of the package, where it passes through the little gap between your fingers, and emerges in one single repellent strand, to ooze out onto your plate. Oh yes, now is probably a good time to mention that you should be leaning slightly forward over the table so that the slender shaft of oleo drops onto your plate and not your pants.

One point of importance—the consistency of the butter is paramount. Actually, it's only really bad if the butter is too hard because it won't come through the tiny hole. Softer is better. It's only too soft to work when it ceases to be solid and crosses over to liquid. If the butter at your table is too hard, just hold it between your legs and let your body heat warm it up.

Try not to practice this trick with our book open on the table in front of you. These pages are not oilproof.

Good luck.

HANGING A SPOON

Forget supposed talents like "singing," "building a sky-scraper," and "curing disease." This "hanging a spoon" skill leaves those others in the dust. Once you know how to exe-

cute this timeless maneuver, the world will beat a path to—and through—your door.

What They See: You pick up an ordinary spoon, and leisurely hang it by its bowl, off of your nose. You may also stick other spoons onto your cheeks and forehead.

What Actually Happens: "What actually happens" is you hang a spoon off of your nose. Really, it's not hard, once you know how to do it.

First, take a look around you. If you find yourself living in a tasteless, low-class dump, Bingo!, there's an excellent chance that you can do this stunt right off. Why? The more flimsy your silverware, the easier it is to perform this trick.

Run past your shiftless mate and numerous, hyperactive children, and head into the kitchen. Push aside the box of Little Debbie cakes and near-empty bag of fried pork rinds, and find yourself a spoon. Wash it.

With the indented part of the spoon's bowl facing you, fog it up by panting on it (this is actually important).

Press the bowl flat up against the end of your nose, push up slightly so the vapor on the spoon and the natural moisture on your nose can "lock," and let go. The spoon should hang there anywhere from ten seconds, to a couple of minutes, depending on how well you've stuck it, and how violently you move your head.

Troubleshooting points: If the spoon doesn't stick instantly, try tilting your head back an inch or so, and give it time to adhere . . . Or use a lighter spoon . . . Or wipe off the bowl and your nose and try again (perhaps a foreign body is standing in the way of your success).

Notes: Use the same technique to attach multiple spoons to your cheeks and forehead—all at the same time. Bob Friedhoffer plays up this spoon stunt in a number of memorable ways. One way: After removing the metal spoon from his face, Bob brings his cupped hand up to his nose, and drops a concealed horseshoe magnet from his palm—although, to the audience, it looks like it fell out of his nose. This nose-magnet apparently explains how the spoon stuck in the first place. Another way: Bob turns a fork so its tines face the audience and sticks that high up on his forehead (if you have a lot of hair, pull it back first). Then, when he removes the fork, he brings both hands up to it, sticks a thumbnail underneath it, and clicks the nail off the fork as he removes it. The illusion? The fork was magnetically stuck to a metal plate in his head.

THE WONDERFUL
TELEPHONE TRICK

Mark performed this stunt thirty times the day he learned it from Mac. It's easy to do, a fooler, and an enormous laugh generator. What more could you ask for?

What They See (or Hear): Your friend Larry is speaking with you on the phone, when he hears a very disturbing side conversation on your end of the line. In the room with you, apparently, is someone who doesn't like Larry very much. This nasty, far-away-sounding Person X keeps shouting out things, like "Are you talking with that dirtbag, Larry?" and "Hang up on that jerk!" Despite the fact that this Person X sounds like he must be standing twenty feet away from you—you are, in fact, Person X!

What Actually Happens: Suppose you're holding the phone in your right hand. Okay, quickly turn the receiver away from you, and move your right arm as far to the right as it will go (as if you were handing the phone to someone who was standing a few feet away from you). At the same time, turn your head left.

Because the phone is turned away and positioned a couple of feet from your mouth, when you now speak, it'll sound (to the person on the other end of the line) as if some unrecognizable voice is talking across the room from you. The illusion is perfect. Now, onto the presentation and the subtleties involved.

For realism's sake, you must "throw your voice" while the person on the other end of the phone is speaking; otherwise, your own voice may give off a telltale flinch, as you "interrupt" yourself.

So while they talk, strike your bizarre voice-throwing pose. When you do this, by the way, keep a tight grip on the phone, otherwise the other person will hear you moving around (trust us on this).

Shout out your obscenity (cursing seems most effective here, although you could also say something like, "Is that Larry? I'd love to do him!"), and instantly jet the receiver, and your head, back to their normal phone-conversation positions. Your friend on the other end will, no doubt, stop his speech dead in its tracks, and ask, "Who the hell is that?"

Offer your apologies for Person X's rudeness, and perhaps whisper a side comment to X ("Yeah, it's Larry. Cool it").

Carry this on for as long as you like. Remember, though, if you don't let your friend in on the gag, he won't know he's been tricked. Instead, he'll just think you've got some numb-nutz in the room with you.

That's the basic "work." On, now, to a neat variation, suggested by *Magic for Dummies* impresario, David Pogue. Call this "The Wonderful Telephone Trick, Speaker Phone Version."

Dial your friend and tell him that you have someone else on the other line, and you'd like to have a three-way conversation. When your friend agrees, pull the receiver about eight inches from your face, and say, "Larry, is this working? I'm on speaker. Can you hear me?" Quickly bring the phone back to your head for his reply. When you hear his, "Yes," pull the phone back eight inches again, and call out, "Okay, Larry, I've got Howard Thurston on the other line. [Pretend to address this fictional third party] Howard, I've got Larry on the phone, can you hear us?"

Hit the basic phone pose, and make Howard "speak." Continue the conversation, listening through your ear piece, pulling the phone back eight inches, and striking the basic voice-throwing pose as often as the situation calls for. You won't, however, be able to keep these gymnastics up for long. You'll be laughing too hard!

Notes: Once you've fooled one person with this, ask them to help you experiment. When you "throw your voice," try shouting, then try speaking in a conversational tone. Which works best for you? In general, we find the conversational tone more realistic, but get feedback on which one you do best. This trick can be helpful in getting you out of a conversation you don't want to be in. Merely "throw" your own name, and say to the person on the other line, "That was my boss. Gotta go!," and hang up. You're welcome. Better do this trick as often as you can now; when picture-phones come into vogue, this stunt will be much harder to perform. This trick was first shown to Mac by big-time TV producer and comedy writer Larry Wilmore.

STRAW FROM NOSE

What They See: She's quite good-looking, the woman sitting across the table from you. This is your first date, so you're really trying to impress her. You're doing all the right things: opening the door of your AMC Gremlin for her, not closing said door on her shin, taking her to the McDonald's in the good part of town, where you even offer to carry the food tray. As a matter of fact you're so gallant that she's almost embarrassed to mention that you forgot to get her a straw for her chocolate shake. Apologizing profusely, you reach up with a flourish (not forgetting to let her see that your hand is empty) to your nose hole and slowly withdraw a straw. Ever the gentleman, you peel the paper covering from the straw and stick it down into her shake, ready for her to suck. She's yours.

What Actually Happens: To do this you need two paper-covered straws. The fatter the straws, the better. It is our milkshake slurping experience that Dairy Queen and McDonald's have the best straws for this. Prior to the presentation, you must first force the paper on one of the straws into a bunched-up "worm" at one end of the straw (see figure 1). Pull this bunched-up paper off the end of straw, but make sure it retains its hollow, tubelike form. This is held unseen behind your right middle finger by your right thumb. Throw away the naked straw; you don't need it. The end of the paper-covered straw is held by your left hand just out of your date's sight below the edge of the tabletop. How you get into this position is no one's business but yours.

Reach up to your nose with your right hand. Make sure that the back of your hand faces your dining companion, thus concealing the little squat paper tube. Under the guise

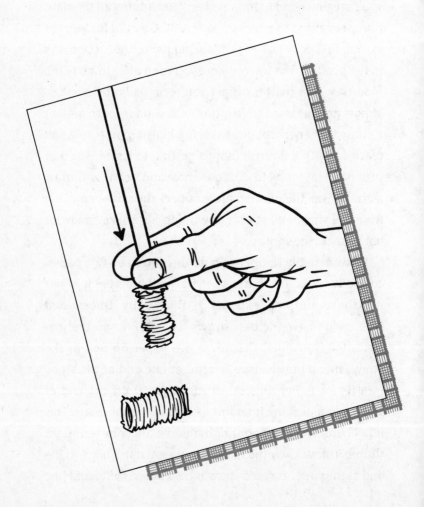

of reaching into your nose, surreptitiously shove the straw paper into your nostril. As soon as the paper is completely in your nose, adjust the position of your right hand so that its palm faces outward and can be seen empty. Then, with the tips of your right index finger and thumb pinch the lowermost bit of the paper and slowly begin to withdraw the paper from your nose. As with most things, it's best not to give it a quick yank; you want the paper to slowly unpleat as you pull, giving the illusion that a solid cylindrical paper tube is being drawn out of your nose. This is pretty darn distasteful looking, so play it up.

Now comes the tricky part. You are going to switch the empty paper cylinder in your right hand for the fully functional straw-in-wrapper held by your left hand. A few things happen in quick succession here, so pay attention! As soon as you feel the top end of the paper pop free of your nostril, your right hand moves a bit faster down in the direction of your lap. When your right hand reaches a point about four or five inches above the tabletop, it comes to a stop and simultaneously lets go of the straw paper so that it continues down and lands in your lap. At the same time, your left hand (carrying its complete straw-in-wrapper payload) comes up to meet your right hand. Both hands now hold the top end of this paper-covered straw. In one continuous motion, move the straw out about eight or ten inches toward the center of the table, where you tap the lower end of the straw on the table, as both hands push the wrapper down to reveal the straw inside. Completely withdraw the straw, and quickly insert it into your companion's drink before she can object.

We should mention that when Mark performs this trick he adds a little touch to the left hand's concealed straw that he feels is a convincer. Prior to the performance he carefully pushes the paper down on that straw too, and then pulls it back up, so that the straw is now covered with a wrinkly paper that will more closely match the look of the wrapper that's drawn out of your nostril. Not being quite as anal as Mark, Mac performs this trick exactly as initially described.

And it must be said that while this is one of Mac's favorite tricks in the book, he did not come up with it. There's this guy, see, and his name is Glen Strange. No kidding. And this is his contribution to the world. And wouldn't you agree the world is a much better place because of Mr. Strange?

One last note before we move on to lesser items; it should be mentioned that this is how both Mac and Mark met their wives. So if you find a woman who actually does think this trick is wonderful, marry her. We did.

SMACK!

What They See (or Don't See): Under the guise of testing a trusting friend's motor skills, you slap him in the face while his eyes are closed.

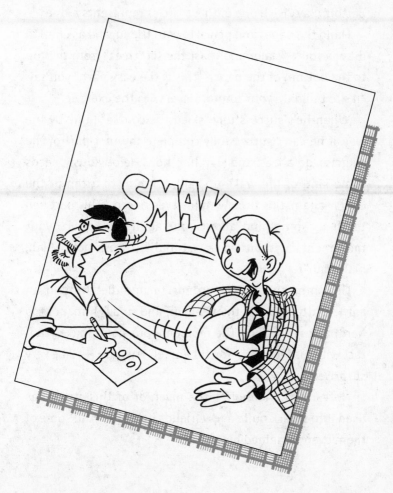

What Actually Happens: For this well-meaning, yet strangely mean, gag, you need a pencil and paper.

Ask your friend if he knows how to ski. Whatever his answer, say that you'd like to test his motor skills based on simple skiing principles, and draw a half-dozen half-inch circles down the center of the paper from the top to the bottom. Say, "Each one of these circles represents a tree."

Hand the paper and pencil to your friend, and ask him to draw a route "slaloming" past the six "trees" from the top to the bottom of the paper. "This is the easy part," you say. "It's to build up your comfort level with the exercise."

When he's successfully "skied the course" (and, by the way, if he can't successfully complete the first part of the exercise, go ahead and slap him now. He obviously needs some kind of life wake-up call), ask him to attempt the course again, this time with his eyes closed. "This part will teach us something about your ability to retrace your movements without visual stimuli" (translation: "Blah, blah, blah").

Give him about five seconds to muddle through an earnest attempt, and then haul off and smack him (not too hard) across the face. The moment your palm makes contact with his face, yell, "You hit a tree!" Trust us: He'll be very surprised.

Notes: Bob Friedhoffer, the inventor of this stunt, has used it to smack quite a few friends in his life. And some of them even remained his friend.

A SINGULARLY "POUROUS" HEAD

What They See: Remarking that the human head is an unbelievably complex series of interconnected pathways, you pour water in your ear and spit it out of your mouth.

What Actually Happens: This trick is physically easy, but the acting required to pull it off successfully will take a bit of work. Take a sip of water from a bottle of water. Pretend to swallow all of it, but retain most of it in your mouth. Raise the opening of the bottle up to your ear. Tilt the bottle as if you're pouring the water directly into your ear hole. Don't really pour water into your ear. You'll look stupid. Before people realize that you haven't tipped the bottle up far enough to actually pour water into your ear, spit the water out of your mouth in a nice thin arching stream. This is where the acting comes in. You need to get the audience to understand that the water you (apparently) pour in your ear is the same water that comes gushing from your mouth. You can help get this across by looking toward your ear as the water is poured in, then shifting your gaze down toward your mouth just as you spit the water out. This is a small point, but attention to the small points is what sets the genius gagster apart from the greenhorn.

You'll notice that we haven't mentioned where you should spit that mouthful of water. You have to decide that for yourself. If you're really worried about what your host thinks, you can spit it into a glass. If you're only a smidgen worried about what your host will think, you can spit on the floor. And, of course, if you're not worried at all, spit directly on your host.

SCALEHEAD

What They See: With your back turned, a spectator selects either a red, black, or blue pen and writes his selection's color on a piece of paper (if, for instance, he selected a blue-inked pen, he'd use it to write "Blue" on the paper). The spectator then sets down the pen and folds up the paper tightly. You face forward, ask for the paper to be set atop your head, and start lightly bouncing on the balls of your feet.

"Hmm," you say, "each of these inks has a different weight to them, based on pigment. Also, each color is spelled with a different number of letters, so a paper with, say, 'Red' on it might weigh less than 'Black.' In this case, though, I sense the weight is somewhere in the middle. I'm certain you wrote the word 'Blue' on this paper." And you're right! The effect can be repeated (at least until the pens run dry).

What Actually Happens: A glance at the pens tells you which one the spectator uncapped while your back was turned.

To prepare, get three different-colored, capped pens that have these qualities about them: (1) They have a brand name running clearly down their barrel (like "PaperMate"), and (2) they have a cap with a clip running off it.

Set them up as follows: For the red and blue pens, make sure their clips point flush to their barrels' brand name; for the black pen, make sure its clip is a quarter turn to the right of its barrel insignia. Get yourself a few scraps of paper, and you're ready to perform one of the most deceptive tricks in the book!

Dump the pens and paper onto the table, as you tell your audience that you're like a human scale. You're so accurate, in fact, you can feel the difference in weight up to one-thousandth of an ounce. Point to the tabled items, and offer to demonstrate.

Explain that when you turn your back, a volunteer should pick up a pen, and write that pen's ink color on a paper. They're then to recap the pen, and ball up the paper. When they're finished, turn around, but don't look at the pens instantly.

Instead, talk about your delicate weighing abilities ("I can differentiate the entire contents of my stomach right now"). After a brief spiel, tilt your head slightly forward, and ask the volunteer to rest the paper on top. Hold it there against your noggin with your hand. Now's the time (while your head is tilted down) to dope out the ink's color.

As you look at the tabled pens, you'll notice that one of the caps doesn't quite line up with its barrel insignia in the way it did when you started the trick; that's the pen that was uncapped and used to write on the card.

Don't blurt out your finding yet, though. Go through your weighing routine, and then announce your decision. When you're proven right, discard the used paper, and let your volunteer go through the whole procedure again. (You still know the distinct starting positions of all three caps, even though you haven't touched them since the trick began.)

Notes: Steve Fearson, who has invented tricks for some of the biggest magicians in the world, originally put a version of this effect on his magicians-only videotape, "Party Tricks." . . . We used only three different-colored pens for teaching purposes in this write-up. If you want to add, say, a green and purple pen to the mix, by all means, do. Why, you might wonder, does one of the pens have to be a quarter-turn off to start the trick? To throw off clever, eagle-eyed spectators. If all the pens matched perfectly, someone might get suspicious. What happens if your volunteer puts back his pen's cap exactly as he first found it? Run.

EATING A FLAME

Wouldn't it save a lot of time if we could eat raw ingredients, swallow a flame, and cook the meal in our stomach? Well?

What They See: You light your lighter, corral the flame in a hand, swallow it (the flame, that is), and cough up smoke.

What Actually Happens: In your left pocket, keep an open baggy filled with talcum powder.

When you're ready to perform, ignite the lighter with your right hand, and get a flame going that's slightly smaller than your fist.

Approach the flame with your loose left fist and pretend to cup the flame—in actuality, you merely ease off the lighter's ignition button, allowing the flame to instantly die out.

Bring the nonexistent flame up to your mouth, and pantomime swallowing it. Grab the lighter in your left hand, and shove it into your left pocket. As far as the audience is concerned, the stunt is over. You've pretended to gulp a flame. Done.

While your left hand leaves the lighter in the pocket, secretly pinch some talcum between your fingers, and bring the hand back out.

Apparently stifle a cough. Bring both hands up to your mouth, and let out a genuine, hard cough into your palms.

The talcum will create a nice "smoke" cloud around your head, "proving" you've eaten fire.

Notes: Bob Friedhoffer, the creator of this effect, used to do it as part of his comedy magic act.

SAMURAI RUBBER BAND

In Las Vegas there is a juggler. HA! In Las Vegas there are a thousand jugglers; there are almost as many jugglers as there are magicians. But there is only one Michael Goudeau. He's the hilarious juggler in The Lance Burton Show at The

Monte Carlo Resort. And this is one of the most powerful
laugh generators in his act.

What They See: Using only a rubber band, you instanta-
neously transform yourself into a Japanese samurai.

What Actually Happens: All you need is a big fat rubber band—the kind that is about a half-inch wide and about one and half to two inches in diameter. The sort that comes on broccoli in the grocery store is perfect.

Ask your friend if she wants to see your impression of a samurai. Despite her answer, you stretch the rubber band over the top of your head so that you're wearing it like a headband, but a tiny bit higher (see figure 1). You want its position to be very unstable. Not like plutonium, but as if, at any moment, the force of its contraction is going to cause it to squirt off the top of your head. Actually, after a couple of seconds that's exactly what you want it to do. You may need to wrinkle your forehead a bit in order to get this to happen. If, after a couple of seconds of brow furrowing, you can't get the band to move, then you need to adjust it to a position slightly higher on your head.

Just as you feel it beginning to move, you shout "Hi-yah!" and strike a samurai pose. The rubber band contracts, expelling itself up to the top of your head, where it automatically traps your hair into an attractive samurai top-knot (see figure 2).

RUBBER CEMENT RETARD

Thanksgiving is a huge holiday at Mac's house, the biggest one of the year for his wife, Jennifer, and him. They usually have about thirty people, mostly magicians, come from all over the country to celebrate and eat with them. Last Thanksgiving Mac asked if anyone had any ideas for this *Tricks with Your Head* book he was working on, and his pal Mark Kalin jumped up from the table and ran upstairs to Mac's office. "I have just the thing for you. You're going to love this." Five minutes later he came sauntering down the stairs, and when the guests got a look at his face, a couple of people spit cranberry sauce, they were laughing so hard.

What They See: You look like a complete doofus. If you've ever had the urge to look like a complete doofus, then this is for you.

What Actually Happens: As the title suggests, you're going to need some rubber cement. You can usually find this in the grocery store school-supply section, or if you're at Mac's house for Thanksgiving, it's in the top left-hand drawer of his desk. Paint this rubber cement in an inch- to inch-and-a-half-wide path around your mouth (by this we mean the outside of your mouth—on your face; don't be an idiot and put any rubber cement in your mouth). Let it dry. Now, turn your lips inside-out and stick them to your face.

There's really no other way to describe this in words, so

take a look at the drawings to see what the heck we're talking about. Your upper lip gets pulled up toward your nose, and your lower lip gets pulled down toward your chin. The beauty of rubber cement is that once it's dry, it only adheres to itself, so if you press your lips down good, they will stay in this pulled-open condition. You can talk while you're

made up like this, but try not to put too much stress on the glue. And, while it's best to set this up in front of a mirror, don't look at yourself too long or you'll start laughing and that will almost certainly pull your lips loose. Remember, loose lips sink shtick.

When you're tired of your doofus fun and want to get on with your life, just reach up and gently pull your lips back into normal position. You can rub the rubber cement off with a dry towel, or your fingers. You'll have a nice red ring around your mouth for about thirty minutes, so it's proba-

bly not a good idea to do this right before you accept your Academy Award on national television.

Two small points, you might want to have a hanky or small towel handy because, with your lips in this wide open position, you've got nothing to keep the saliva inside your mouth where it belongs. And make sure it's rubber cement, for, while we're sure smearing your face with Elmer's glue would be funny, the effect is just not the same as this. Oh, you'll look retarded all right, but for a completely different reason.

TOOTH PICK

What They See: Someone freely chooses any tooth in your mouth and when you open your mouth, that exact tooth has a big black X marked on it.

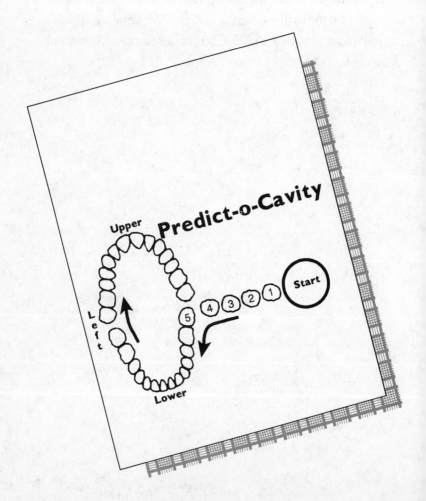

What Actually Happens: There's bit of preparation necessary here. Photocopy this dental chart. Look in the mirror at your teeth. Look back at the chart. Look at your teeth again. Figure out which tooth in your mouth corresponds to the tooth on the chart closest to the bottom end of the "P" in Predict-o-Cavity. Dry that tooth off with a couple of squares of toilet paper. If putting toilet paper in your mouth grosses you out, sell this book. Now get a black or dark brown eyebrow pencil and draw an "X" on that dry tooth. You're all set.

Show the dental chart to your friend. Ask her to put her finger on the "START" circle. Point at the circle of teeth. Explain it to her. "These are all the teeth in my mouth. There are twenty-eight. These four off to the side are my wisdom teeth. They're over here to the side because I've had them removed."

Ask her to think of any number between five and twenty-eight. She can name the number out loud or not. It doesn't matter. Have her count out her number (starting on wisdom tooth number one) into and around the circle of teeth, following the direction of the arrows. Tell her to keep her finger on the tooth where she lands. Now say, "To totally randomize the tooth selection process, count that same number of teeth BACKWARDS around the circle of teeth, starting with the next tooth. Don't go back into the row of wisdom teeth, just keep going along the circle of teeth that are actually in my head." She should end up pointing at the tooth that matches your actual marked tooth. "So you've randomly selected a tooth?"

Pretend like you're trying to help her figure out exactly which tooth she's stopped at. "Let's see, it's in the upper teeth. And it's on the right side. And it's the third one over from the center." Now open your mouth and raise your upper lip, kind of like Elvis, so that she can see for the first time the big black X on the very tooth she "randomly" selected.

SLAP! SLAP! ALL FALL DOWN!

One night at Dalt's restaurant in Burbank, California, our friend Eric Mead held Jim Steinmeyer, Mike Caveney (voted two of the most influential magicians of the twentieth century), and Mac (never voted anything) mystified for at least half an hour with this enigma. It was a very memorable night. It's really fun to be fooled for that long. We like it and maybe you will too.

With that in mind, we'd like to try a little experiment right now with you, dear reader, but we need your cooperation. We'd like you to try this trick out on yourself right now. Please don't skip ahead and read the explanation. Just read up until you're told to stop; then look at the drawings and try this thing out. Give yourself a few tries. You'll get this to work for you, and (hopefully) you won't know why or how it works. Trust us—that's a seriously cool feeling.

What They (and you, if you're really trying this) See: Get a smallish, thinnish piece of paper. A sheet of notebook paper is the right amount of thinnishness, and you can tear a rectangular piece about one and a half by two inches off of it (that's the right amount of smallishness). The dimensions and thickness of the paper don't have to be exact; that night at Dalt's, Eric used half the credit card receipt. One of the short sides of the paper has to be completely straight (no jagged tears).

Fold the piece in half lengthwise. Sit at a table. Stand the piece of paper on its narrow end about a foot from the edge of the table (see figure 1). Sit up straight. Throughout the next rapid series of actions, keep your right hand's fingers straight and together, and your palm completely flat and rigid. With this flat right hand slap yourself on your right

cheek. It's actually more like you stroked your right cheek downward and slapped it at the same time—kind of like you're trying to generate static electricity. And then in quick succession, slap/stroke your left cheek with that same rigid right hand of yours, then bring down your right hand (pretty briskly) and point your hand at the piece of paper. The paper should fall over.

That's it; those are the actions. If you do it right, that paper WILL fall over. Study the drawings, try it again, and for goodness sake, don't read ahead and spoil the wonder you will experience when this finally works for you! It's pretty quick: Slap! Slap! Point! Fall. To get the right balance between slapping and stroking your cheek it might help if you pretend you're a guy in a really goofy aftershave commercial.

Here are some things to think about as you continue to try this. We have been told that if you have a two-day growth of beard, this will work better, but our extensive research shows that women with no facial hair (and boys, too) can learn to do this just as easily as anyone. Please don't think that this is a joke. It's not. It really works. We are not trying to scam you into slapping your face for no reward. We know that we have given you no cause to trust us, but please, trust us anyway.

This is worth devoting a bit of time to. If we were there in person and could do this for you, you would want to learn it. And don't take our earlier mention of static electricity to indicate that that's how this works. Neither should you take this denial as proof positive that it doesn't work like that. At least for a few more sentences we're not saying how it works. Every time we do this for anyone, his or her first inclination (especially if they already know the dollar bill moving trick on p. 36) is to think that we just blew the paper over, and the hand motion has nothing to do with it.

Those people are wrong. They eventually find out they are wrong when the trick works for them, and we're standing on the other side of the room.

If you're trying this over and over, and still not getting it to work, carefully go over the instructions step by step. It's important to use your right hand, and to slap your right cheek first, then your left. It won't work if you strike your left cheek first. As a matter of fact, THERE'S something for you to puzzle over; what possible difference could it make which cheek you slap first? Okay, keep trying this and don't read the explanation. READ NO FURTHER.

What Actually Happens: We're not kidding. Try this before you read any further. Get it to work. Then try to figure it out on your own before you take the weaselly action of letting us simply tell you. Okay. We assume you've tried this, gotten it to work and you have a theory or two as to why it works, and you're simply reading this explanation to confirm your hypothesis. Well, you're right, it is air current. The teeny tiny breeze your right hand generates as it travels from your left cheek to the table top is enough to topple the paper. So simple it's almost disappointing, isn't it? That's why you should NEVER, EVER tell anyone why this works. Unless you get something really great in return.

PING-PONG BALL ON NOSE

This is a stunt designed to show what amazing hand-eye-nose coordination you possess.

What They See: Exhibiting a regulation Ping-Pong ball, you toss it gently into the air. As it descends, you tilt your

head back and the ball lands on your nose, where, instead of ricocheting wildly away, you manage to make it stay— balanced on the very tip of your proboscis!

What Actually Happens: If you hang around real professional magicians a whole bunch, there are a few genuine secrets that you can unearth. The main insight you will come up with is that magic is much, much simpler than you originally thought. Almost all good magic methods boil down to Velcro, coat hanger wire, gaffer's tape, or (as is the case here) rubber cement. Get a bottle of rubber cement, a Ping-Pong ball, and your nose. Go to your secret, private, rubber-cement-applying chamber and completely coat your nose and the Ping-Pong ball with rubber cement. Let dry. The rubber cement will be undetectable to any observer who does not try to Eskimo-kiss you.

When you're ready to demonstrate the stunt, exhibit the Ping-Pong ball at your fingertips and gently toss it into the air. Tilt your head way back. Keep your eye on the ball as it descends and contrive to make it land on your nose. Due to the characteristic stick-to-itself property of rubber cement, the ball will remain perched on the exact place where it hits your snout. Play this up. Keep your head tilted back and dance a bit from side to side as if you're balancing the ball there on your nose with great difficulty. To conclude, either reach up and swiftly snatch the ball off your nose and bow to the ovation, or expose the gaffus by raising your head up and saying "thank you" with the ball now perched like a clown nose in an impossible gravity-defying position.

SWALLOWING A GOLDFISH

Back in the 1930s, Matt Schulien was creating a sensation in his Chicago bar by swallowing goldfish. That's right. Each night patrons would gather around the stout bar owner, watch him dip his hand into a tank, stuff a squirming fish into his mouth, and gulp it down like a whiskey shot. Schulien's laughing patrons couldn't get the tip money on the counter fast enough.

Schulien's stunt became so popular that college kids around the country began imitating it. Swallowing goldfish, in fact, became a craze, much the same way as dancing The Lindy Hop is today, or lancing your eye with a fork (p. 186) will be in the future. The only problem with these college kids' live goldfish consumption? These kids were stupidly doing the real thing—cruelly munching on these wriggling (and unsanitary) fish; Matt Schulien had only been doing a magic trick. The bar owner/magician had fooled everyone with the illusion that he was eating live fish.

What They See: Like Schulien, you pluck a fish from its tank and stick it in your mouth. Before you swallow the poor creature, your audience can see its tail thrashing around through your pursed lips. Gulp. You're now a legend.

What Actually Happens: To prepare, take a potato peeler, or pairing knife, and cut yourself a thin, goldfish-sized sliver of carrot. Wastefully toss the carrot into the garbage, thoughtlessly leave the peeler or knife for someone else to clean, and stick the carrot sliver into your pocket. You're set.

During your daily travels, conspire to find yourself next to a tank full of carrot-colored fish, and secretly get the pocketed sliver into your loosely cupped right hand. Look mischievously at the tank, and yell out to any nearby people, "Hey, want to see something peculiar?" (You may have to yell this a number of times before anyone takes you up on your offer.)

While your audience is forming, eye the fish as if you're trying to make some decision about one of them. When it seems like you've made your choice, shove both your hands into the tank and chase the fish around briefly (not too much chasing, though, or you'll ruin the trick and stress the fish).

Apparently grab a fish, and bring your cupped hands above the water's surface. Let the excess water drain through your fingers for a split second. (You don't want to swallow more fish water than you need to.)

Bring your hands up to your mouth, and stuff the carrot in—allowing a half inch or so of its tip to protrude from your mouth.

Clandestinely jiggle the body of the carrot with your tongue, so its exposed "tail" wriggles around spasmodically. Grin, chew, swallow. Wipe your mouth disgustingly with your open palms.

Notes: This stunt works best when you have a half dozen, or more, goldfish to "choose" from. Why? If you "grab" a fish in a sparsely populated tank, it'll be obvious to onlookers that you didn't remove a genuine fish (Tank owner: "Hey, I only have two fish, and there they both are. What the hell do you have in your mouth, magic boy?") . . . You're presenting this as a stunt, or an entertaining demonstration of bona fide LIVE fish eating. Be natural about it (or as natural as you can be with something like this). Forget overly theatrical movements . . . Just remember: Flash the "tail" briefly. Don't draw the "wriggling" out . . . After you down the "fish," you'll probably want to rinse your mouth out, since you did, in fact, drink a trace amount of fish tank water. Remember what W. C. Fields said.

PICK MY NOSE! PICK MY NOSE!

What They See: Asking someone to concentrate on your face, you say, "You know that whole, 'eyes are the window of the soul' thing is greatly overrated. You can tell much more about people by examining their teeth. Or their nose. Or even their ears." As you remove an envelope from your pocket you continue, "This is an extremely important item. You'll know why in a moment. I want you to make a conscious decision. In your mind I want you to select a part of my face: either my teeth, or my nose, or my ear. You can change your mind as many times as you like, but when you've settled on one of those items—my teeth, my nose, or my ear—let me know."

When, after hours of intense thought, they finally say that yes, they've come to a decision, you open the envelope and extract a paper-covered straw. "Now I want you to touch the part of my face you've chosen, but wait! Not with your dirty finger, but with this amazing, and sanitary, divining straw." They take the straw from you and gently place the end of it on your nose. "My nose. How fascinating. You had a free choice. No one influenced you to select my nose? Please peel the paper covering from the straw. You'll find some words printed there on the straw." They do so. The straw reads, "THANKS FOR PICKING MY NOSE."

What Actually Happens: To do this amazing feat of mental prophecy you need the following items:

one or more spectators

a paper-covered straw

an envelope large enough to hold a straw

a piece of paper the same color as the envelope, but just slightly smaller (you can cut up a second envelope to get this)

a pen that will write on a plastic straw (an extra-fine point Sharpie works great)

a nose

an ear

at least one tooth

On the address side of the envelope write, "THANKS FOR PICKING MY TEETH."

On one side of the piece of paper write, "THANKS FOR PICKING MY EAR." Put the piece of paper into the envelope so the writing side doesn't show.

Trying not to wrinkle it too much, carefully slide the wrapper about halfway off the straw. On the exposed portion of the straw write, "THANKS FOR PICKING MY NOSE." Slide the paper back up over the straw, covering up the writing; try to make it look like the straw wrapper is intact. Put the straw into the envelope, and the envelope in your pocket. Make sure you place the envelope into your pocket so that you can withdraw it later without exposing the writing on it.

You're now covered with a plausible prediction for any of the spectator's three choices. Go back and reread the opening paragraph and see how what you say is structured to make any of the three predictions seem like the only prediction.

When performing the trick you proceed as described, making sure that when you withdraw the envelope and set it on the table in front of you (or simply hold it in your hand) that you don't expose the writing side to your onlookers. If they select your teeth, you say, "Remember I said that the envelope would be important? Well, turn it over." There is your written prediction thanking them for picking your teeth.

If they touch your ear, you say, "Remember I said that the envelope would be important?" Then you withdraw the piece of paper from the envelope (making sure that they can see that there are no other predictions inside the envelope) and turn it over to reveal the prediction for your ear. Obviously if they pick your nose, you simply proceed by revealing the straw prediction as described in the first paragraph.

If you like this trick (and we do), you might want to join us in thanking David Regal. He's a fabulous magician/animator who adapted this trick from an old trick called "Mental Choice." We think David's version is boss.

A FUNNY POSSESSION

What They See: You assure a spectator that you have an image of their selected card inside your head, only you can't quite seem to locate it. "Don't worry, though" you say, "I have a little spirit who possesses me, who runs around inside me and helps me find images I've misplaced." So saying, you summon up the spirit—which reveals itself to the spectator as a little arm jutting out of your ear. And in the hand of the little arm? A playing card. A playing card that matches the spectator's selection in value and suit.

What Actually Happens: To prepare, you'll need a few things: a doll's arm large enough to stick awkwardly out of your ear, glue, a miniature playing card, and a normal-sized deck.

Glue the minicard into the doll's hand, and stuff it in your right pocket. Get the normal-sized duplicate of the minicard to the top of the deck, and you're ready to perform the trick.

Ask the spectator for a number from one to ten. Whatever number they pick, begin to deal cards off the top of the deck, into a pile, until you reach the number. Pretend, suddenly, you made a mistake: "Oh," you say, "I wanted you to do the dealing so everything's fair and square." Pick up the dealt-off pile and put it back on top of the deck. Slide the pack over to the spectator. The card you secretly want him to select is now at the number they just named (i.e., if they called out "Six," your force card is now at a position sixth from the top of the deck). Remind the spectator of his number, and have him deal down to that card and remember its identity (without anyone else seeing). Have him reassemble the entire deck and shuffle it.

Take the cards back from him and place them into your left pocket (the one without the doll's arm). Start to make wild guesses as to the identity of his card. An example of what you might say: "Was your card red? No? Was it black? Yes! The ace of spades?" (You, of course, know that his card was the, for example, nine of clubs, because you forced him to take it.) "No? It wasn't the ace of spades? I thought you said it was black? Listen, fella, there's no such thing as a red ace of spades, so if you tell me your card is the ace of spades, it must be black!" (This, naturally enough, is double-talk and nonsense—essential ingredients in any magic trick.)

You continue: "Okay. Maybe it's me who's screwing up here. Maybe I'm not getting a clear picture of your card. But I know someone who can help me lay a hand on the picture of your card." Here's where you patter about your being possessed by a little spirit who helps you locate misplaced images inside your head.

Tell the spectator that you want to go into a trance so you can summon up the spirit, but it would help if he (the spectator) freshened his mental image of the card. "I want you to look at your card again," you say, dipping your hands into your pockets, as if you were searching for the deck.

Bring out the deck from the left pocket, and come out secretly with the doll's hand in your closed right fist. When all the spectator's attention is on locating his selected card, surreptitiously shove the doll's hand into your ear, so the minicard faces the spectator.

When he finds his card, he'll look up at you and laugh. Say, "I think my spirit already found it."

Notes: Bob Farmer, one of North America's most beloved lawyers, invented this trick to use on defendants during cross-examination. You can find loose doll arms at doll hospitals. If not, go to craft shops. If that doesn't work, buy a cheap, hollow plastic doll at a toy shop, and snip its arm off at the deltoid. Continue altering the doll's arm until it fits snugly. Do not, under any circumstances, alter your own head to do this trick. Always make sure the doll's arm is serving your needs, and not the other way around.

More Notes: When Mac does this trick, he follows the preceding routine, but he uses the hand from a GI Joe. It's not one of the miniature GI Joes they tried to pawn off on kids a number of years ago; it's a real, full-sized GI Joe, one who could sleep with Barbie. These GI Joes have hands that can be pulled right out of their arms with no pain or discomfort to the doll. Plus, the wrist nubbin attached to the hand is the perfect size to wedge into your ear hole. And instead of a miniature playing card, Mac tears the index corner from a duplicate of the force card and sticks it into Joe's Kung-Fu Grip.

NOSEBREAK

In the world of head magic, this is a standard, a classic, a stunt you will pull for the rest of your life, and cause all in your wake to groan, "Urrrggggh. . . ."

What They See: Complaining that your sinuses are stuffed, you wrench your nose in an effort to clear them. "Crack!" An unnerving bone-breaking sound rings out. "Okay," you exclaim, "that's better."

What Actually Happens: For the trick to work, you must have a normal to long thumbnail. Those nervous readers

out there who've bitten their nails down to the sub-nubbin are out of luck; they'll actually have to break their nose to get the trick to work.

To perform, first drone on about your stuffed sinuses. Then, cup both of your hands over your nose. Under the cover of your palms, wedge a thumbnail under one of your top, front teeth. The next two actions happen simultaneously.

Twist your cupped hands slightly to the right (or left), as if you're forcing your nose cartilage in that direction. While that happens, snap your thumbnail forward, producing a painful sound.

Bring your hands down, sniff loudly, and go on with your life.

A REALLY GOOD NOSEBLEED GAG

What They See: You're watching television and you sense that your mom is about to come ask you to take out the trash. When she comes in the room, you're holding a piece of paper to catch the drops of blood that are dripping with

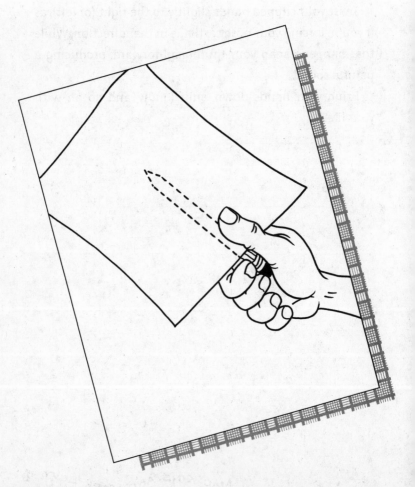

a steady "Pop! Pop! Pop!" from your nose onto the paper. She makes your sister take out the trash.

What Actually Happens: Get a nice white sheet of typing paper. Dot the paper with a few tiny drips of runny catsup. Place the sheet of "bloodstained" paper over a pencil and hold it as in figure 1. Hold the paper under your nose and pretend to catch drops of blood on the paper. The sound of blood drops plopping onto the paper is achieved by pressing your thumb firmly against the paper (and pencil), and sliding the paper forward in a series of tiny undetectable jumps. Each tiny jump produces a loud "pop." You may have to experiment with different pencils to find one that works.

Resist the natural temptation to clutch your nose with your free hand. You don't want people to think that hand conceals some sort of blood-dropping device. Just keep the paper below your nose and make believable nosebleed noises (argh and ugh are both serviceable) and the illusion will be so astonishing that people will believe they really see drops of blood falling through the air from your nose.

THE OLD HEAD-BANGS-INTO-
THE-DOOR GAG

What They See: You're working for the United Nations, and it's your job to lead the ambassador of an aggressive country up to the podium, so he can address the general assembly and declare war on the world. While you're walking him

through a back corridor, you race ahead so you can catch a door that's swinging shut. Bam! The door hits you flush in the face, after which you spit out a few teeth. The ambassador, delighted with your buffoonery, tears up his prepared war declaration and, instead, leads the assembly in an impromptu Beatles sing-along.

What Actually Happens: The door hits the front of your shoe, and you spit out Chiclets.

Practice walking into a closed door so that your foot (it doesn't matter which one) is about three inches in front of the rest of your body. Get it? You're striding purposefully into the door and propelling the tip of your shoe into wood (or metal) just before your face would get smashed. In point of fact, your lovely face never actually makes contact with the door. Instead, when your shoe makes loud contact, you snap your head back, as if it's been hit. To enhance the illusion, you might also toss your arms about, as if you're trying to regain your balance.

When you think you can carry off this violent part of the trick, complete your preparation by secreting a couple of white Chiclets in your mouth (if you have black teeth, use the black Chiclets instead).

To perform, race ahead of your friend, and get to the door first. If it's swinging toward you, so much the better. Put up your hands, as if you're going to push the door forward, but let your foot get out a few inches ahead of you and absorb the blow. Do your staggering fall-back move.

If the door is closed, open it, but do it in a way so that it appears you've miscoordinated the door's opening and your stride past it (maybe the door stuck for a split second? Wink). In this case, too, kick your foot subtly into the base of the door, and overact.

As your friend jogs toward you to see if you're all right, lean your head close to your hand and spit out the Chiclets. He'll be fooled for a heartbeat, and then he'll probably kick your butt.

Notes: Naturally, you can do this gag by performing the head-hit part, and leaving out the Chiclets-spit. But never, never, never, do the opposite. That is, don't perform the Chiclets-spit, independent of the head-hit. If you do, you'll just seem very weird.

A TRICK WITH ALEXANDER HAMILTON'S HEAD

What They See: You can make the portrait on any piece of paper money smile or frown at your whim! That's right, just by following these simple instructions, you can make your

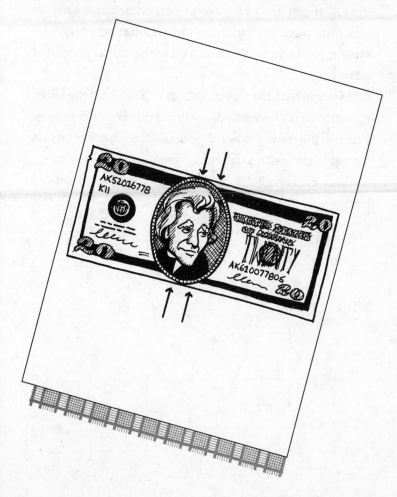

favorite paper money politician actually appear to be changing facial expressions! All it takes is two folds!

What Actually Happens: Look at the drawing. Make nice crisp valleylike folds right through the center of your chosen politico's eyes. Make sure the two folds are parallel to one another, and perpendicular to the long sides of the bill. If you don't know what perpendicular means, go look it up. Actually, if you don't know what perpendicular means, you're probably doing this with a dollar instead of a hundred.

Once you have the nice crisp folds in place, hold the bill by its ends and tilt it slightly away from you. Hamilton frowns! Tilt the bill slowly toward yourself and his expression changes; he's smiling right up at you!

This works on all U.S. currency, even the new big-headed kind.

THE IMPALING STRAW

Why do magic tricks involving the human head so often end up as mock-mutilation stunts? (A purely rhetorical question.)

What They See: You grab a drinking straw, position it against the soft flesh under your chin, and thrust up. Instantly, the straw penetrates the underside of your head and comes up through the floor of your mouth. A bloodless impalement!

What Actually Happens: You accomplish this horrific miracle through the use of what we in magic's inner circle call a "gimmick." In this case, the gimmick is a small piece of drinking straw—about an inch to an inch and a half in length—which you've clandestinely snipped before the trick begins. This gimmicked piece of straw must match the color and thickness of the full-length straw you'll be using when you perform the trick.

Let's say you plan to freak out your friends over lunch at the local burger joint. Before you push through the glass doors of the restaurant, stick the gimmicked straw piece into your mouth. Then go about your business, ordering lunch and so on. You'll find that you can talk quite naturally with the straw in your mouth. (Indeed, it might shock you to know that most magicians these days walk around with straw pieces in their mouths and can conduct full stage shows without tipping the gimmick. However, Teller, of

Penn and Teller fame, finds it rather difficult, so he keeps silent to ensure that the gimmick won't roll out. Now you know why . . .) Tuck the straw on the side of your mouth or on the middle of your tongue, whichever feels most comfortable.

STRAW

When the conversation lulls, grab a full-sized straw in your right hand and say, "Watch this!" Hold the bottom part of the straw with your knuckles facing the audience and your right thumb stabilizing it in back. Position the top of the straw flush against the soft underside of your chin.

Now, lightly push up on the straw with your right hand. Rather than the straw moving, you'll find that your hand slowly slides up the base of the straw. Let your hand rise up about two inches before you stop. From the spectators' point of view, two inches of straw have disappeared up into

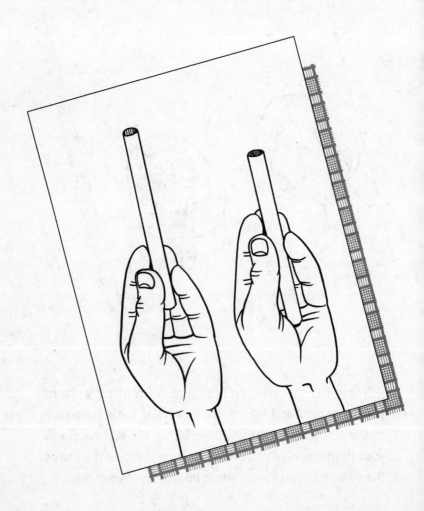

your skull (rather than down into your hand, where they really went).

While you're executing this move, use your tongue to move the gimmicked straw piece in your mouth into a standing position, right behind your lower front teeth. The gimmick must be standing at precisely the spot in your mouth where the full-sized straw is "penetrating." Difficult? Not really. Fifteen minutes' practice in front of a mirror should put you at the world-class level in performing this sleight.

Finally, open your mouth. Go ahead, do it. Perhaps you'll feel a bit dopey the first few times you do this trick, since you'll know you're concealing two inches of straw in your hand and trying to pass off a little nubbin of a straw as the impaling weapon. But your spectators won't be able to keep from roaring with laughter (or horror) at the perfect illusion before their eyes.

To extricate yourself, reverse the procedure: Close your mouth, and slide your hand down the full-sized straw before "pulling it free" from your head. You can either continue lunch with the straw tucked away in your mouth or subtly spit it into your napkin as you wipe your face. If your spectators ask to see into your mouth while the gimmick is still there, try the line that Kevin James, originator of this trick, uses when challenged: "Eat me."

Notes: Some performers hold the top of the full-sized straw against their chin with their left fingertips as they perform the penetration sequence. Those fingers further mask the fact that the genuine straw really isn't moving.

If you're performing in a store that provides plastic lids on their drinks, you may want to use this variation on the penetration sequence given to us by Minneapolis magician Jim Flagg: Put a straw into the drink lid, but don't push it all the way down to the bottom of the cup. Keep the genuine straw erect in the tight hole of your drink's cover; then position your chin over the top of the straw and push down with your head. Now, instead of your hand moving up the straw to effect the penetration, the straw will move down into the cup, giving the same illusion. At the trick's conclusion, pull the straw free of the cover and cup.

Bonus Tip: If you like Chinese or Japanese food, you can do the same trick with a wooden chopstick.

FINGERTIP EYEBALLS

Sorry, you can only perform this trick if you have a friend. If you don't have a friend, forget this one. Instead, page back and learn some of the more disturbing stunts—things like eating glass (p. 33) or punching your thumb through your ear (p. 46)—and cultivate an "eccentric" personality for yourself; that way, you'll have justification for your lonely existence. You still won't have a friend, but you'll, at least, be smug and condescending about it.

What They See: You rest a thoroughly shuffled deck upright on your skull, so the cards' faces are visible to everyone but you. One at a time, you deal cards down to the table. Each time your fingertips contact an ace, you call it.

What Actually Happens: During a party, interrupt all the rowdy, sexually charged side conversations by announcing you'd like to do a card trick (in the magic field, this is known as "getting the audience on your side"). Ask for a deck, and stress that it be shuffled before you even lay hands on it.

While waiting for the cards, seat yourself at a table so the lower half of your body is obscured from view. Get a previously coached friend to sit beside you (remember, this friend must be a flesh-and-blood person, not imaginary! You can't, for instance, have some dreamed-up, benevolent werewolf, who protected you as a child, aid you here). This friend must also have her lower half shielded from view.

When you're handed the deck, position it on top of your head so it faces the audience, and stress that you've never laid eyes on these cards. Assure the audience, however, that you needn't use the eyes in your head to "see" the value of each card. You can actually view them with another part of your body—the fingertips.

"Yes," you continue, "while my mom was pregnant with me, she tried to keep healthy, so she ate a bushel of carrots each day. Well, I don't know how much her carrot consumption improved her eyesight, or mine, but they sure helped the sight in my fingers. That's right. My fingers can see! Their vision isn't great—they're horribly nearsighted—but it's functional. Let me demonstrate."

As you hold the deck upright with one hand, use the other to start dealing cards to the table, while you mumble, "This card isn't important, or this card, or this one . . ."

By this point, your friend has inched closer to you, as if she's trying to get a better view of the spectacle happening atop your head. Actually, she's only moved so she could surreptitiously rest her foot immediately next to yours.

Each time your friend sees an ace appear at the face of the deck, she secretly—and lightly—taps her foot to yours. "Ah!" you exclaim, as you feel her gentle pressure below the tabletop, "my fingers see an ace, they're pressed right up against one, and they're asking me to keep it." Deal the ace off to the side, as a keeper. Continue this way until you've reached all four aces, or until the audience has turned away in indifference, or until your hidden game of footsy has inflamed your passion so greatly that you toss away the deck, shout "Forget card tricks—give it to me baby!" and leap upon your confederate.

Notes: Aces, of course, are only one card value to "see." As long as you've coached your friend beforehand on what to react to, you can "see" a Royal Flush, a four-of-a-kind called for by the audience, or a selected card that your friend saw while you were out of the room. When we say that you and your friend must have your lower bodies obscured from view, we don't mean that you both must be unnaturally flush with the table's edge, so it cuts your stomachs like you were baked hams. Be realistically close to the Formica, that's all. Remember, the audience has no idea that you're being tipped below the table. To them, all the action is happening above your head. Suppose your friend isn't in a position to sit next to you? Use your imagination on other ways she can signal the information to you: a slight finger movement, a flare of her nostrils, and so on. Just don't make it obvious, and make certain she's in your line of vision throughout the trick—but don't stare or steal suspicious, psychopathic side glances at her.

SWALLOWING A KNIFE

This was a favorite of Bert Allerton's, the Chicago close-up magician who performed it more than half a century ago.

What They See: During dinner, you gleefully swallow a butter knife.

What Actually Happens: Secretly drape a napkin in your lap, and sit yourself about eight inches away from the edge of the table.

Grab a dull knife, such as a butter knife, and position it about four inches from the table's edge. Announce to your buddies that you're still hungry, and approach the knife in this way:

Bring your right palm down onto the knife, parallel with the table's edge, obscuring the cutlery from view. Your left hand waits just below the edge of the table to receive the knife, as you drag the knife toward you with your right hand. Let it fall past your left hand into your lap. No one, naturally, will see the knife drop, because your right hand and arm are shielding the view. No one will hear it, either, because of the napkin (the napkin also prevents the knife from falling to the floor).

Without hesitating, bring your hands stiffly up to your mouth, as if they're still holding the knife between them. During this simple deception, be sure to move your thumbs in behind the four fingers of each hand, mimicking the action your thumbs would take if you really were lifting the knife.

Tilt your head back. Open your mouth wide. Put the supposed bottom end of the knife into your mouth.

Using the right hand, help push the nonexistent knife into your mouth by slowly drawing your fingertips against your left palm. At about the point when your right fingertips contact your left palm, pivot the right wrist out to the right, and continue your fictional pushing—as if you repositioned the right hand so you could "eat" every last bit of the knife.

Once your right fingertips reach your lips, close your mouth, lower your hands, and make gulping noises—perhaps slapping your chest in the process, to "aid digestion."

Look satisfied, and continue with your meal.

Notes: For comic buildup, performers often salt the knife while it rests on the table . . . Never use a sharp knife, since you're running your hands over it, and it falls into your lap (Ouch!). If a dull knife isn't handy, use a spoon. If laying a napkin in your lap isn't convenient, make certain to

squeeze your thighs tightly during the drop (Ouch!)...
Some non-napkin-draping people end the effect this way:
They let the knife slide between their thighs and stand in
silhouette. Then they bend over and pretend to reach
between their cheeks, and slowly produce the knife from
there. We disagree on the effectiveness of this breech repro-
duction. Mark thinks it's hard to do convincingly, but Mac
thinks the trick isn't worth doing unless you finish by
extracting the knife from your butt.

HYPNO HEAD

Mark: I can't let you do it, Mac. I can't let you release this routine to the general public. This stuff is way too good. I know some professional magicians, and a bunch of stage hypnotists, who regularly use this material. It's a betrayal of all we stand for . . .

Mac: I don't care. This routine is dynamite, and I want our readers to learn it and use it!

Mark: But we'll be drummed out of the magic societies! And the hypnotists will menace us on the streets with their little sleep-inducing hypnotic wheels! I won't let you do it! Give me that pencil! Arrrgghh . . .

Mac: Aaaaarrrgggghhh . . .

(Sounds of a struggle)

What They See: You apparently hypnotize a volunteer, making it impossible for him to open his eyes until you command him to. Then you make it impossible for him to stand up from a chair!

What Actually Happens: We're sorry to inform our power-hungry readers that at no point in this routine do you actually hypnotize your subject, or attain a Svengali-like domination over his mind. No, you cannot will him to strip naked and run in place, step off a high ledge, or paint your house (including primer).

Yet, while you'll have no direct control of your subject's mind, you will be using his body's natural physiology against him. (Sounds promising, right?)

For the first part of the routine: Ask your volunteer if he's ever been hypnotized before. If he has, forget about our trick for the moment and instead try to find out if he's been given a posthypnotic trigger word you can use to make him bark like a dog. If he won't tell you the word, call him a baby and continue with the routine.

If he's never been hypnotized, explain that there are many popular misconceptions about the hypnotic state. For one, being in a trance is not like being asleep, but is more like being highly focused on a single object or idea. Ask him if he's ever lost track of time while writing, for instance, or while working at a favorite hobby. That feeling is very similar to the feeling of hypnosis. In fact, you can explain, he's almost certainly put himself in a hypnotic state through his focused activities without even realizing it.

Tell him that you're quite a hand at hypnotism and would like to conduct a short experiment in some "light hypnosis." (The word "light" encourages your subject's cooperation by calming his fears of hypnotic zombification.)

Ask your subject to sit up and look straight ahead. Talk some more about the power of single-minded focus and the relaxation that accompanies it. After a moment, ask him to direct his gaze to an imaginary point on the ceiling—a point close to him, almost directly overhead. Tell him that as he stares at this point, he should keep his face pointing straight ahead; only his eyes should look up. If he follows your directions, his eyeballs should roll tightly upward in his sockets.

Now ask him to slowly close his eyelids while he continues to stare at the imaginary spot. This is the key to the first part of the routine: As long as your spectator continues to look up while his eyes are closed, it is physiologically impossible for him to open his eyelids. (Try it yourself.)

This first "feat of hypnosis" will be more impressive if you play it up. Tell your subject to take deeper, slower breaths. Tell him to concentrate on the high spot. Ask him to visualize a skyline in his forehead, which gives him a clear view of his focal point. Reassure him that he's doing a great job of concentrating on the spot. Speak in a low, soothing monotone like the fake hypnotists you've seen on TV and in movies.

After this buildup, ask him to continue his focus on the spot—continue staring at it physically and mentally—and then give him the command to open his eyes. Instantly follow this command with the suggestion: "But you can't open your eyes. They're sealed tight. You're focused on your spot, you're concentrating intently on that spot, you're relaxed, and you can't open your eyes!"

After a few beats, tell him he'll soon be able to open his eyes. (By the way, if you happen to know how to safely invert your own eyelids, so onlookers see veiny pulp instead of your pupils, this would be a great time for it. Do your eyelid thing, muss your hair, suck in your cheeks, and prepare to give your subject a nice surprise when he opens his eyes.)

Finally, ask him to lower his gaze so he's looking straight ahead, get his mind off the focal point, and open his eyes. Congratulate him on his superior powers of concentration.

For the second part of the routine: Ask your volunteer to sit back in his chair and relax. (Don't omit this part. His position in the chair is important to the success of the trick.)

Tell the subject that closed eyes can hasten a descent into trance, but they aren't absolutely necessary. You now wish to demonstrate "waking hypnosis," in which the subject's eyes remain open.

Ask your volunteer to fold his arms tightly across his chest, like a rap star or someone sitting in judgment. Tell him that this position signals the brain to release alpha waves, which helps to firmly fix one's concentration. (If someone questions this bogus explanation, look agitated, feign a full body tremor, and scream, "Prove me wrong!" If you can, you may want to do that eyelid inversion thing again.)

Suggest to the subject that he is growing temporarily weak. His strength is running out of his body. He's so weak, in fact, that you can keep him from standing up using only a single finger.

Stand directly in front of your seated subject and press your index finger firmly into the middle of his forehead. Command him to keep his arms tightly folded and his feet flat on the floor ("Don't break the trance!"), and rise. He'll be unable to.

The reason? In order to get up out of a chair, you must be able to throw your head and torso forward, as you slide one foot forward for balance. As long as you subtly prevent your spectator from doing these things, he'll be forced to sit in that chair the rest of his life (or until you develop an arthritic forefinger, whichever comes first).

After eight to ten seconds of struggling, ask the spectator to relax again. Tell him that when you remove your finger, the trance will be broken, and he'll awaken refreshed and happy. Count to three, and take your bows.

Notes: In the can't-open-his-eyes part of the routine, it isn't necessary that your subject's eyes spin back in his head like slot machine cherries. If it's done properly, you can still fully see his eyes, only they're focused higher than usual, as if your spectator were in a neck brace and were watching a bird flying overhead.

When Mark performs the can't-stand part of this routine, he subtly presses the tips of his shoes against the tips of the spectator's shoes, making it harder for him to slide his feet forward.

In either part of this routine, if the spectator defeats the "hypnosis" (he opens his eyes or stands), tell him that he's fighting you, that he stinks as a hypnotic subject, and that he's probably limiting his potential for growth as a human being. Move onto another spectator, who, after your tirade, will probably be more likely to cooperate.

EYE IN THE BAG

What They See: You remove your eye and plop it into a paper bag. One at a time, you allow your audience to reach in, feel the moist eyeball, and go "Yuck!" When everyone has

gone "Yuck!," you reach into the bag, and slap your eye back into its socket. The bag is empty; your hands are "clean."

What Actually Happens: A skinned grape mimics your eyeball, and a secret assistant in the audience steals the grape for you. Here are the details:

Get yourself a nice, plump grape, and delicately peel off its insecticide-soaked skin. Toss the skin. Put the grape in a small paper bag. Tell your secret assistant how he's to help you (more on this in a moment). You're now ready for the show!

Pretend to remove your eye by bringing a cupped hand up to your socket, shutting tight your eyelid, and "withdrawing" the eye in your fist (actually, your hand holds nothing).

Gently place the make-believe eye in the bag.

"I have to keep my eye in this dark bag," you tell the audience, "because direct light will dry it out. But if you want to feel my eyeball, come up one-at-a-time, I'll let you have a touch." While you're delivering this patter, remember to keep your "eyeless socket" shut.

Let each person stick his hand into the bag and feel the "eye." The last person to stick his hand in is your secret assistant. When he sticks his hand in (and goes "Yuck!" just like everyone else), he quietly keeps hold of the grape when he's finished. No one, of course, realizes he's helping you with this trick, so no one will be watching his actions closely. After he's done the dirty work of stealing the grape, he'll rejoin the audience.

"Okay," you say, "time to put back my eye." As you reach into the bag and pantomime replacing your disembodied eye, your assistant ditches the grape. Where? He can eat it, stick it in his pocket, drop it down his shirt, roll it under the table. Everyone will be watching you, so—short of tossing the grape into the air and catching it in his mouth—your assistant can do whatever he likes to get rid of it.

Up to this point, no one will have been really fooled by the trick. They realize they weren't feeling your eye, and they "know" you still have some eye-gimmick inside the bag. Here, though, is where you get 'em good.

Once your "eye is back in its socket," blink a few times as if you're getting some dirt out of it. Say, "That's better. Won't be needing this eyeball carrying case anymore." Rip open the bag, allowing everyone to see it's empty. Continue tearing it into small pieces; ball them up; and, carelessly toss it. Your audience will be stunned.

Notes: This wonderful stunt is the work of Mark Setteducatti, the super-talented, professional inventor of magic tricks. When Mark originally devised "Eye in the Bag," he didn't use the eye-removal part of the trick. He merely showed the audience a closed bag and said he'd found an eyeball. The spectators then felt the grape; his confederate stole it; and, he showed the "eye" had vanished. If this creepier, spartan handling appeals to you, by all means, use it.

When Mark Levy performs this trick, he adds an old, but effective, gag to the eye-removal part of the routine. As

Mark's right hand apparently tosses his eye into the bag, his left hand makes it appear as if his tossed eye hits the bottom of the bag with a thud. How? Mark's left hand holds the bag—thumb on the outside, fingers on the inside—and he snaps his left middle finger off his forefinger; that violent movement creates a loud rustling, and visible jarring, in the bag.

HEAVY HEAD

What They See: To demonstrate how unreliable human senses are, you ask a volunteer to hold an empty bowl atop her head and shut her eyes. You then lightly place your forefingers on her eyelids and your thumbs on her cheeks, as safeguards against you attempting any sleight of hand.

In a hypnotic voice, you command her to feel the bowl getting heavier, as if a twenty-pound cannon ball were weighing it down. Soon the volunteer giggles because, indeed, the bowl is getting darned heavy. Yet when you remove your hands and ask her to open her eyes, the bowl is empty.

You try the experiment again, only this time, the volunteer experiences no change in the bowl's weight. "Oh, really," you sneer, as you remove your hands from her head. When she examines the bowl this time, however, she discovers a physical manifestation of her thoughts: A shockingly large loaf of bread overflows the bowl that's been in her hands the entire time.

What Actually Happens: In a nutshell: Although the volunteer thinks you have both your hands touching her face, you, clever devil that you are, are touching her with only one. The heavy bowl, and appearing bread, happen courtesy of your secretly free hand. Here are the details of those maneuvers.

To make the bowl feel heavy, do this: Bring both your

hands up to her face, with the forefinger and thumb of each hand foremost. Once she closes her eyes, pull your left hand back, and let your right arm do the work of both: Lightly lay your right forefinger on her right eye; your right middle finger on her left eye; your right thumb on her right cheek;

and, your right ring finger on her left cheek. (Your right pinkie dangles flaccidly off your hand.)

Use your left hand, then, to reach up over her head and press down in the middle of the bowl, feigning a substantial weight. When you're ready to end this part of the rou-

tine, bring your left hand back to her face, and remove both your left and right—making sure you "withdraw" them in the same, outstretched forefinger-thumb combo that you used when you started. Ask your spectator to open her eyes. To her, everything looks the same.

To load the bread in the bowl: Before you begin the trick, jam one end of the loaf into your back pocket. During the performance, and after freeing up your left hand the second time, reach behind yourself, secure the bread, and delicately place it into the bowl.

Notes: You can only perform this trick, of course, for a single spectator (unless you want to turn the whole thing into some romping, French farce; if that's the case, then, hell, bring in a tour bus of people to watch it). Brilliant Brad Stine created this gem of a trick, including the unique idea of four-point contact on the spectator's face. Brad, though, had some help here: The pressing-down-on-the-bowl idea came from genius mentalist Michael Weber; the four-point finger configuration described in the text came from Stella Levy (Brad's configuration, which might suit you better, left his forefinger dangling); and the end-of-the-trick-load idea was Mark's (who finally found a use for that loaf of bread he keeps in his back pocket).

What They See: On the count of "three," you vanish the victim's coin, just as she's about to close her fingers around it. To get the coin back, you tell her she'll have to implore a power higher than yours. You instruct her on how to hold her hands

in prayer position, while she wails, "Please Jesus, send me some money!" In the blink of a deifying eye, the coin seems to drop out of the heavens and plops into her waiting hands.

What Actually Happens: Borrow a quarter, and have your victim make a unique mark on it, so she'll be able to later identify it.

Take the coin from her, get her to hold her palm out flat, and say you're about to conduct a test of her reflexes. Tell her that on the count of three, you want her to close her fingers as quickly as she can around the coin.

Now, before describing the following sequence, let us ask you a question: Have you ever tossed a dart before? Yes? Good. The arcing motion that you use to toss a dart is the same motion you're going to use now to display—and vanish—the coin. Here goes:

Holding the coin in your right fingertips, quickly arc your arm up near the top of your head, and slowly drop back down to a position just above the victim's palm. Say, "One."

Repeat the sequence, swinging your arm up near your head, and dropping back down. Say, "Two."

As you arc your arm up and back a third time, actually place the coin on top of your skull and leave it there. Continue back down, as you calmly say, "Three." The spectator, primed from the first two kosher steps in the sequence, will be anxious to grab at the nonexistent coin. Show your hand shockingly empty.

Patter: "Gee, I guess your reflexes aren't fast enough. Before you could grab your coin, it vanished into some otherworldly dimension. You know how to get it back, though, don't you? Prayer."

Have the victim bring her hands up to chest level, and clap them together, as if she were reciting a prayer. Ask her to shout, "Please Jesus, send me some money!"

When her coin fails to rematerialize during this first cry, lightly grab her wrists, and open her praying hands into more of a bowl shape, or like a book that's just been opened. Ask her to repeat her lamentation, as you continue to stabilize her wrists. Tell her to put more feeling into her cry.

If she's looking up, tell her to be more humble, and stare into her hands. When she complies, bow your head an inch or two, causing the secreted coin to slide off your scalp, and into her cupped hands. Her prayers have been answered.

Notes: You might wonder, "Won't she see me leaving the coin on top of my head?" The answer: No, that's what practice is for. By repeating the get-ready-to-grab-the-coin sequence, you lull your spectator into thinking that she's seen all you got in the first two swings. When the third step comes up, she's busy watching her own palm, because you've challenged her to a test, and looking at your head has nothing to do with the test. Your job: Practice placing (not tossing) the coin on your head, with as little hitch as possible.

You'll also need to practice the dropping of the coin into her hands. An easy way to do that? Pick an imaginary spot on your bed, stick a coin on your head, and practice hitting the spot. If you get bored, pretend it's World War II, you're in a bomber, and you're over Tokyo. When you can hit your target ten times in a row, you've won your captain's wings. Why do you need to hold your victim's wrists during the reappearance? So she doesn't move them, and so that she sees that your hands aren't involved in the coin's reappearance. The methodology of this trick is old, but the spiritual dress for this effect was given to us by corporate magician Bill Goldman.

One More Note: Six-time "Magician of the Year" winner, Michael Ammar, uses the same object-on-the-head principle in a different trick. When performing for children, Michael points to the middle of the room and asks if anyone sees the invisible cookie tree growing there. "Yeah," he says, "instead of dropping apples like an apple tree, it drops cookies." So saying, Michael grasps a young volunteer's hands and helps her cup them. Almost immediately, then, he dips his head forward and allows a secreted cookie to fall from his head into her waiting hands.

THE SOUND OF NOTHING

What They See: While the last of the dinner dishes are being cleared, you ask a tablemate to participate in a quick audiology experiment. "Each time you hear me break one of these toothpicks," you say, "point to the sound."

You pick up the first toothpick, and snap it near her right ear. Your volunteer, of course, points to her right. "Correct," you say, as you drop the toothpick halves to the table. You repeat the test, this time near her left ear. Naturally, she is correct again.

On the third leg of the experiment, you snap the toothpick directly in front of her face. Your volunteer points straight ahead, right at your hands. "You heard it break here?" you say, "That's interesting." Without a false move, you slowly spread the fingers of both your hands, showing no toothpick at all. "Either the toothpick vanished," you crow, "or there never was any sound to hear!"

What Actually Happens: There are two secrets at work here: (1) You never really pick up the third toothpick, and (2) you flick your thumbnails together, simulating the sound of the toothpick breaking. Here, then, is what you do in performance:

Toss a handful of unwrapped toothpicks—perhaps a dozen—on the table.

Follow the routine as written, until you get to the third toothpick. Reach into the pile, pretend to grip one, and leave it there as you lift your hand. Immediately bring your hands together, following the same prebreaking motions you used in the first two go-arounds.

Once the fingertips of both hands overlap, jam your right thumbnail under your left thumbnail (this reads painful, but it's not).

Snap your thumbs forward, so the left nail flicks off the right one. The toothpick-breaking auditory illusion is strong here, so be confident that everyone is fooled. Freeze your hands in postbreak position, and wait for the spectator to point to them. Reveal.

Notes: Again, another marvel from the brain of Brad Stine.

THE TOAST

Here's a funny, interactive toast for you to use the next time your sister is marrying a boob. Get the groom up to stand beside you as you address the assembled reception attendees. Hand him a glass of champagne and say, "This is the

initiation into our family. If you can follow my actions precisely, I predict great happiness for you and my sister. If you fail, your union is doomed." You should have everyone's attention.

Extend your glass full of champagne straight out in front of you. Groom-boy follows suit. Bring your glass back toward you and then out to your right; then back toward you and out to your left. Again, he follows your actions. Next take a sip from the champagne. He does the same. What he doesn't know is that you only swallow a tiny bit of your mouthful, retaining the majority of the liquid in your mouth. He of course swallows all of his; I mean, why wouldn't he? Again you extend your glass out away from you and then back, all the while secretly holding a mouthful of champagne. Now raise the glass toward your mouth and spit the retained liquid back into the glass. The groom cannot do this.

You've ruined his life, but saved your sister's!

Hooray!

STUCK ON YOU

What They See: You, rascal that you are, grab the chewing gum from your mouth, and stick it onto a friend's shirt sleeve. Presumably, the friendship is now over. But wait! When you remove your hand from his arm, the gum has vanished. Slowly, you begin to chew again. The gum, apparently, has reappeared in your mouth.

What Actually Happens: First, use your favorite method for getting a piece of gum into your mouth. Chew it (like a human, not like a cow; were you raised in a barn?).

Second, eye an uptight, weaselly friend, and push the now-glistening gum to your lips, using your tongue and jaw muscles for guidance.

Third, raise a hand to your mouth, and pretend to remove the gum, while you, in fact, lightly suck it back into your mouth.

Fourth, matter-of-factly press your partially closed hand to one of his sleeves, as if you're smearing the sticky gum to it. An important note: Your rodentlike friend, strange as this might seem, may not want you pressing saliva-covered gum to his sleeve. He may struggle. Be prepared to forcefully grab his retreating arm with your free hand, so you can stabilize it.

Fifth, after a few seconds of fictional smearing, yell "Wait!" (making certain that the hidden gum doesn't tumble from your mouth in the process), lift your hand, and show the gum gone. Your friend will, doubtless, be relieved.

Sixth, draw silent attention to your face by giving a look exactly like the look you'd give if a piece of prechewed gum appeared metaphysically in your mouth. Start to chew, opening your cake hole widely enough to let him catch a glimpse of the bewitched gum.

Notes: We've walked you through this trick like it's one big joke. Ha! Ha! Ha! But to make the stunt work, you must put in a brief, but serious, moment of practice. When you reach up to "take" your gum, you must make it look like you really did remove it from your mouth. We urge you to stand in front of a mirror and actually remove your gum three or four times, so you'll be able to duplicate your actions during the "sleight." Attention to detail, like we're asking you to do here, can spell the difference between you looking like a hero ("That was great! You're so cool!"), or a douche bag ("That sucked! You're a douche bag!")....

In case we terrified you with the preceding warning, and you're having trouble "looking natural" while removing the gum, here's a point to remember: When you normally pick up a small object, your four fingers obscure the object, and your thumb, from view. That's the movement you're trying to duplicate while you're apparently grabbing your gum. Too often, when we teach this trick, we see people unnaturally snapping their hands closed, while their thumbs stick awkwardly out. We hate these people and their awkward thumbs. . . .

This trick was invented by Eric Mead, a professional magician with smoothly functioning thumbs.

SEEING THROUGH A BODY

In this trick, you'll learn about two things very dear to any working magician: One is a principle, misdirection; the other is a technique, how to force a card. Be forewarned, though: If you screw us by flagrantly flaunting these ideas,

or performing them poorly, you'll die a slow and agonizing death through poisoning.

That's right. As you've turned each page to reach this point in the book, trace amounts of a print-based poison have been loaded onto your fingertips. And don't try and wash them clean now, it's too late.

Every time you stuck your finger in your mouth, picked your nose, or scratched your butt since you picked up this book, you have thrust the poison deeper within your system. There's no way back for you.

The poison coursing through your bloodstream now is a "smart" poison—it reads the chemical changes in your system and acts accordingly. If the poison senses that you're tipping "misdirection" for a petty reason, or it feels you butchering a "force," it will exact a horrible, swift, fatal penalty on you. We are absolutely not kidding about this.

What They See: While your back is turned, an audience member turns a selected card face up and sits on it. You ask her to open her mouth, so you can stare down through her body cavity. After some humorous byplay about her intestines and such, you announce the name of the card.

What Actually Happens: Somehow spot the identity of the top card of the deck, making sure that no one notices you doing it; this is the card you'll later "see."

Ask a spectator to give the tabled deck a cut, so that the two halves wind up next to each other. Pick up the original bottom half of the deck, and drop it across the original top half, saying, "Let's mark the spot where you cut" while you do it. The deck now sits in a cross formation on the table, with the force card resting uppermost of the lower half. Draw attention to a chair, any chair, in the room.

Patter: "I want you all to study this chair. Take a look at it. Rap your knuckles against it. Any trapdoors, mirrors, or light-reflecting devices attached to it? Take a moment to make certain it's ungimmicked." This little playlet you're creating by drawing attention to the chair is both entertaining and misdirecting—that is, it's taking "heat" off of the deck, where the true funny business of the trick is going on.

Once the spectators are convinced that the chair is normal, walk over to the deck and cleanly remove the top half. Point to the half that remains on the table, and say, in a commanding voice, "Remove the card you cut to when I turn around. Under no circumstances do I want to see the face of that card."

Turn away, and wait for the spectator to follow your direction. She, of course, is taking the original top card of the deck—the force card, the one whose identity is known to you—only she, and the audience, doesn't realize this. Ask her to turn the card face up, drop it on the chair seat, and sit on it, so its face is obscured. When she's done, face her.

"Okay," you say, "I'm like a doctor. I've studied the human physiology so thoroughly that I can see clearly through the chambers of the heart and every twist the intestines take. Let me prove this to you."

Ask the "patient" to lean her head back and open her mouth. Stare down into her gaping maw, and crack all the appropriate, and inappropriate, jokes. "See" the card, and announce its name.

Notes: There are lots of ways to take this routine. For instance, you can put a paper napkin over your subject's chest, have a cup of water nearby, and do dentist shtick. . . . This trick was originally performed by Lou Derman, the late head-writer of *All in the Family*. A big cheese at The Magic Castle in Hollywood, Bruce Cervon, recommended it to us.

And famed children's book author Sid Fleischman performs a wonderful trick where he also, apparently, looks inside the human head. After getting the spectator to pick a card whose identity Sid secretly knows, he brandishes an ordinary drinking straw, sticks it in the spectator's ear, and says, "I'm seeing your thoughts, right now. Yes, there's the card you're thinking of, only its back is toward me. Can you mentally revolve that image of your card please? Got it!" He then names it. . . .

Remember the poison.

HEAD CANDY

What They See: You lay out five hard candies—each a different color. "I want you to select one of these," you say to a spectator, as you point to the candies, "but I don't want you to just reach down and grab one. That would be a crass move on your part. I don't know how you were raised, but where I grew up, you had to share. As a matter of fact, in my house we had a kind of silly game that ensured we'd be fair in dividing up candy like this.

"The game was called, 'One divides, the other decides.' In it, one person—say, my brother—would pick out any two objects, in this case candies, and the other person—say, me—would pick which one of the two I wanted to keep. Understand? That way, my brother had to be fair when he selected those two candies, otherwise I'd take the best one and leave him the crappy one. Let's play that game now, but we're going to do it so we keep on eliminating candies until there's one left. You start. Pick two candies, and I'll pick the one we eliminate. Then we'll switch roles."

True to your word, you follow the childhood procedure four times, alternating roles, until four candies are eliminated, and one is left for him. "Good," you say, "that candy's yours. You can start sucking on it if you like." You wait until he pops it in his mouth. You continue: "You know, it's interesting that, even after conducting our game—a game where we both had a number of random choices—you'd pick that red candy. Why do I say that? Because, before we began, I had a premonition of which color you'd chose. I, in fact, licked my prediction. That's right. I licked one of the candies lying in front of you." And so saying, you stick out your tongue: there, sitting disgustingly, smack-dab in the middle of your tongue, is a splotch of red candy. Your spectator spits his prize out.

What Actually Happens: Don't worry. This is a hygienic trick. You don't actually gob the candy (otherwise it would appear all sticky and unappetizing and the spectator would never choose it). Like all the seemingly disgusting or dangerous tricks in this book, this one only appears questionable—the actual method is positively benign.

To prepare, you'll need to take a trip to the supermarket (you can ride in the cart). Once there, grab yourself a bag of hard candies, making sure that you receive five, or more, different colored candies for your money. Then have someone wheel you over to the sleepy aisle housing the food coloring. Purchase a small bottle of coloring whose contents match the color of one of your hard candies (they don't have to be identical shades of the same color; close will do). When you get your bounty home, daub a spot of coloring on your tongue. Now you're ready to perform.

At your performance site, lay out five candies of varying colors. Set up the premise, as we present it in the "What They See" section, until you get to the point where you conduct the childhood "fairness" procedure. That procedure is rigged. Here's how you can conduct it so the spectator always ends up with your predetermined, "force" color:

The spectator goes first and picks two candies. You choose one to be eliminated. Make sure you don't eliminate the "force" color. Simple.

You then switch roles for the next round. You pick two candies. Make sure you don't pick the "force" color as one of your selections; that way, the spectator can't possibly eliminate it. Again, simple.

Continue this way, switching roles for two more rounds. As long as you never touch the "force" candy, your spectator can't eliminate it. At the end, when there's one candy left, it will be the "force" candy—the one you wanted him to "choose." Deliver your licked-prediction lines, and stick out your tongue.

Notes: Why does the picking-procedure work? Mathematics—namely, Roy Baker's PATEO Principle (Point-At-Two-Eliminate-One). That's all we're going to tell you. (We're here to teach you magic, not math, Professor freakin' Algebra. Keep the protractor in your pants.) The idea of predicting candy with a splotch of color on your tongue is Ken Sands's; the use of the mathematical selection process is Mac's; the notion of dressing up that selection process as a kids' game is Michael Weber's; the spit-prediction dodge is Mark's. . . .

When Mark is in a non-food-coloring situation, he takes a duplicate-colored candy and sucks it—revealing that candy as his prediction. It's not as viscerally strong as the "spit" presentation, but it'll do in a pinch.

BREAD SNOT

What They See: You're double-dating with the new couple who's moved into your neighborhood, because in an ill-founded bout of neighborliness you invited them out "to get to know each other." It becomes obvious during the salad course of dinner that you have nothing in common with this twosome, and you never ever want to see them again. Here's what you do:

Begin to sneeze. "Ah, ahh, ahhh . . ." In a near panic, you frantically scan the tabletop and grab the first handy item, a slice of tasty sourdough bread. Quickly bringing it up to your nose, you release your pent-up sneeze into it. ". . . Choooo!" Oblivious to their looks of detestation, you now hand the phlegmy, dripping, repulsive bread slice to your wife, and with a cold stare, issue the chilling command, "Eat this." She looks demurely down at her lap, takes the bread slice and silently, but pitifully, begins to eat it. If the crappy neighbors are still there when she finishes the bread, you might want to reconsider; maybe they're worth knowing after all.

What Actually Happens: This depends on the old switcheroo. Unbeknownst to your audience you've spread a slice of bread with some butter, or marmalade, or other vaguely snotty substance and laid it (snot side up) on the napkin in your lap. Chat on with the neighbors, nodding and pretending to listen to their discussions of bermuda versus fescue, or whatever inanity they're talking about. Then start your sneeze noises, "Ah, ahh . . ." Pretend to scan the table, then quickly (before anyone has time to offer you a tissue) seize the most tissue-soft product there, a fresh piece of bread. Bring it up to your nose and release a huge, powerfully loud, sneeze into it. Wipe your nose on the bread, then bring the bread, with both hands, down into your lap. Leave the real snot-piece there and pick up the fake snot-piece and bring it up to the tabletop.

While your hands are making this switch, your face is providing the misdirection to cover it. After the sneeze, squint up your eyes, shake your head in a blubbery sort of way, and make some exaggerated postsneeze noises. Keep this up only long enough for your hands to travel back up to the tabletop with the switched-in piece o' bread. At this point your neighbors are probably smiling politely to spare you any embarrassment for your incredible faux pas, but when you present this befouled piece of bread to your wife and command her to eat it, the mood will take a very dark turn. And if she acts as if you might haul off and whack her one if she doesn't comply with your wishes, whoa boy, the air will become icy indeed.

Of course, you don't have to make this a two-person stunt. You can simply look at the (apparently) soiled bread slice, shrug your shoulders in a sort of "what the hell" manner, and start chowing down on the mucus-y goodness yourself.

BIG BEN

What They See (and Hear): Exhibiting a simple wire coat hanger with two lengths of string tied to its corners, you announce that this is your latest invention. "That's right," you say, "this deceptively simple gadget is actually a tele-

portation device. It will transport you directly to London." Find a volunteer who wants to take a trip. Coax him to stand on a chair. Instruct him to wrap the free end of each string around each index finger. Then get him to firmly insert the end of his string-wrapped digits into his ears. Tell him to swing the coat hanger so that it knocks into the chair leg. His face will register his delight as he hears the distinctive sounds of Big Ben chiming the hour.

What Actually Happens: There is no trick to this; simply follow the preceding procedure and it just works. Actually he doesn't have to stand on a chair for this to transpire. The reason you have him do so is that the longer the string, the deeper the tone he'll hear. Plus, you should know that the more firmly he inserts his fingers into his ears, the louder the tone's volume. Don't overdo this last point, however; if he pushes his fingers too far into his ears, the only place he'll be transported is to the hospital.

HOW TO MAKE THE AIR IN YOUR LUNGS CHANGE PLACES WITH THE AIR IN A BALLOON

If nothing else, this trick wins the "longest title in the book" award. But don't worry, it has a lot more going for it than that. It is the creation of the hilarious Canadian comedian David Acer, who kindly gave us permission to include this gem.

What They See: You blow up a balloon, holding the nipple closed with your fingers. Then you take a deep breath. Suddenly your body convulses; you exhale, and then release the air from the balloon. "Did you see what just happened?" you ask. "The air in my lungs changed places with the air in the balloon!" Somehow they don't believe you. You offer to repeat it, "And this time I'll prove it." Again you inflate the balloon and hold it closed. Now you borrow a cigarette, light it, and take a big deep drag from it. Once more your body convulses, and you exhale. No smoke comes out. You loosen your grip on the balloon and smoke pours forth. The air in the balloon DID change places with the air in your lungs!

What Actually Happens: Get a big round balloon and some fine talcum powder. Put a bit more than a teaspoon of the powder into the balloon. You're all set.

When you're ready to spring this on your audience, bring forth the balloon, blow it up, and hold it, nipple end up, out to your side. Take a deep breath and hold it. Contort your body in just the way you would were you really causing the air in your lungs to change places with the air in the balloon, but try not to shake up the balloon. You don't want to disturb the powder too much. Exhale audibly, and then release the air from the balloon. Because the nipple of the balloon is pointed up, no powder escapes. Say, "Did you see that? The air in the balloon changed places with the air in my lungs!" Act all excited.

"Oh, you don't believe me? Okay, I'll prove it." Again blow up the balloon and hold it out to your side, but this time hold it with the nipple pointing down. Borrow a cigarette, light it and pretend to take a big drag from it; really just breathe in deeply through your nose. Do those same body contortions you did before, only this time make sure that your movements "inadvertently" cause you to shake up the balloon a bit (this distributes the powder). Exhale audibly. No smoke. Now release the air from the balloon (keeping the nipple pointed down), and what looks to be smoke issues forth. Try not to blow this "smoke" onto anyone; the tiny white spots and the scent of fresh baby powder just might give the trick away.

FRENCH FRY UP NOSE

What They See: Holding a french fry up to your nostril, you give a huge audible sniff, and whoosh! the fatty, salt-loaded tuber gets Hoovered™ up your nose.

What Actually Happens: There are two ways to suck an entire french fry up your nose. This is the one that doesn't hurt. Here's what you do: Pick out a nice crispy fry that's just a bit shorter than your middle finger. You might think you'd want a really rubbery, grease-laden one to lubricate its sinal journey, but you don't—you want a stiff one.

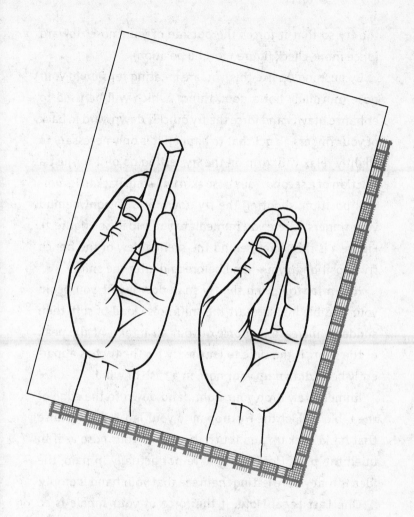

Grip the chosen one at the tips of your right middle finger and thumb so that the fry is parallel to your fingers (see figure 1). Hold the fry up to your nose, but don't stick it into your nostril. The top end of the fry actually touches the outside of the right nostril hole (see figure 1 again). Push up on the fry so that it forces the outside of your nose upward (once more, check figure 1 for the position).

By pushing up like this, you are creating tension in your nose (normally not a good thing), which will be used to enhance gravity and force the fry quickly downward in back of your fingers. To get that to happen it is only necessary to slightly relax your grip on the fry, letting go of it for just a fraction of a second. Your nose skin will snap back to its normal position, shooting the fry down out of sight behind your fingers, where you immediately regrip it (see figure 2). Figure 3 is the secret behind-the-scenes view of the french fry's position in your hand before and after the sniff.

Just prior to letting the fry snap downward, you begin your audible inhale. Start the sniff noise kind of soft, then suddenly increase the force of your air intake. At the peak of the snort is the time to let the fry fly. The fry has apparently been drawn up your nose in a rush of wind.

Immediately drop your right hand down to the edge of the table and let the fry drop in to your lap. Instantly raise that hand back up and touch the side of your nose as if to quell the pain. Hopefully you're not actually in pain; the idea is that you're letting them see that your hand is empty.

One Last Legal Note: If the force of your inhale is so strong that it actually sucks the fry up into your brain we are not responsible for any damages (including funeral costs).

BLOW HOLE

Applied to other parts of the body, this trick might appear obscene. But when used on the nose, it's clean enough to do for any grandpappy or cleric fortunate enough to be seated at your table.

What They See: You blow your nose into a handkerchief, which rises a shocking and comic six inches from the force of your toot.

What Actually Happens: This effect must be done while you're seated, with a table shielding your lap from your spectators' view.

On your lap, hide a long pencil (six to eight inches) and go about your normal business. By no means should you stare suspiciously at your lap, or rest your hands there and nervously fidget with the pencil. For goodness' sake, show some restraint.

To perform the trick, you must conceal the pencil behind your handkerchief or napkin so that it's on the side of the cloth closer to your body. You can get the pencil into position naturally by feigning a sneeze, pulling out your handkerchief, and then lowering it to your lap, or by simply placing your napkin directly on your lap as if to catch crumbs. Either way, you now have the pencil hidden behind a cloth you can sneeze into.

Pretend a sneeze is coming on—by all means, ham it up—and lift the handkerchief-with-concealed-pencil up to your face. As you position the handkerchief to cover your nose, secretly work the end of the pencil into your mouth, about half an inch under your upper teeth. Most of the pencil will be hanging straight down, with one end in your mouth and the other end pointing toward your lap.

You're now going to do two things simultaneously (magic can be a tough field!): (1) Blow a mighty toot through your nose, as if clearing it, and (2) use the muscles of your lower jaw to slowly lever the pencil into a horizontal position. From the audience's perspective, it will look as if your sneeze has caused the hanky to slowly rise from the force of your blow.

When you're finished blowing, use your jaw muscles to lower the pencil, grab it with both hands through the cloth, and drop your arms near the table's edge, but over your lap. To draw attention from the handkerchief, do a few exaggerated sniffles, which will pull the focus back toward your head. Loosen your grip on the handkerchief, allowing the pencil to fall secretly and silently into your lap. Dab your nose again with the cloth and toss it aside.

Notes: Make sure the handkerchief and pencil are over your lap once you've finished your blow. If they're too close to the table, the pencil might click off the table edge and make you the laughingstock rather than the star of the occasion.

Surprisingly few magic tricks involve nose-blowing. This is one of them.

What They See (and What Actually Happens, Too): "I don't know, Mark, maybe I shouldn't compete in the Heptathlon in the upcoming Olympics."

"Oh dear, Mac. Why won't you be able to compete in the Heptathlon in the upcoming Olympics?" Mark logically responds.

"I have Dog Jaw."

"Dog Jaw?" Mark says. "What's Dog Jaw?"

"You've never had Dog Jaw? Oh man, are you lucky," Mac answers. "It's incredibly painful. I mean your neck gets all stiff, and then the nerve on the side starts to pulse." Here Mac strokes the side of his neck indicating the source of his torture. "It's such a weird thing. And the reason they call it Dog Jaw is . . . well, just feel this," Mac says as he turn his head and extends his neck out for Mark to feel the amazing oscillation going on just below the surface of his skin.

As Mark starts to reach to touch his ailment, Mac suddenly turns and snaps at his hand like a crazed pitbull, barking ferociously, "RUFF! RUFF!!"

Mark practically collapses, and then punches Mac in the neck.

While we are practical jokers of immense genius, we are writers of mediocre faculty; therefore, we cannot convey with the force we wish to just how funny this is. To simply say that you snap viciously at the unsuspecting rube's approaching hand and make a loud barking noise falls far short of the impact this gag has. Just remember to be as serious as possible about having Dog Jaw and your description of it. You really want them to be intrigued.

Mac's friend Dean Cameron says that you have to give this "Farley Commitment." What he means by this is that the late Chris Farley's commitment to a joke was just consummate. You must do the same here. Once you have them concerned, and their curiosity aroused, you then do a complete about-face and become as vicious and as mad-dog-like as possible when lunging at them.

Go forth and scare the bejeesus out of someone.

EYESCREAM

Between us, we've probably read over five thousand books of magic tricks, and you know what we've found? They all contain this dramatic line: "This next trick alone is worth the entire price of the book!"

Perhaps the ruling magicians' societies issue a style sheet requiring this sentence, or perhaps they send out muscle men to ensure that the line finds a place in each book. (Possible punishments for leaving it out? A dented top hat? A set of Chinese Linking Rings horseshoed around the unfortunate magician's throat?)

Whatever the reason, we at *Tricks with Your Head* wish to uphold this time-honored tradition. So here goes.... This next trick alone is worth the entire price of the book!

(By the way, we do hope you paid for this book. If you checked it out at the library, or even worse, shoved it down the front of your pants at some bookstore, you'll never be able to do the tricks as well as if you put down hard money to buy a copy. It's all about commitment . . . But back to our trick.)

"Eyescream" has a distinguished lineage. Mac has performed it before nineteen million people on NBC-TV, and those magical gods Penn and Teller thought so highly of it that they included a version in their best-selling book, *Penn and Teller's How to Play with Your Food*. Are you, dear reader, worthy of performing it? Are you ready to learn one of the greatest gag tricks of all time? If so, read on.

What They See: Over dinner with a few friends, you stab your eyeball with a fork, causing white liquid to spray across the table.

What Actually Happens: If "Eyescream" did involve actually stabbing a fork in your eye, the instructions for the effect would end right here. However, as you can see, they take up another five hundred words, so something other than genuine orb-popping must be going on. You don't, in fact, lance your eye; instead, you puncture the foil top of one of those half-ounce plastic coffee creamers that waitresses and waiters dispense from the big waist pockets of their smocks.

So the first step in presenting "Eyescream" is to sneak one of those little creamer containers into your lap. How? Either cop one from the table or grab one elsewhere in the restaurant when you excuse yourself to go to the bathroom. (Note: We magicians are always heading off to the bathroom, but we never have to go. We've trained our bodies to reuse the toxins and waste materials normal people expel. Instead, we use our time in the bathroom to stack decks, secrete rabbits, steal coffee creamers, or in other ways prepare to astonish spectators.)

However you obtain the creamer, don't immediately launch into the trick when you resume your seat. Hang out a bit, talking, eating, shooting the breeze. You want your audience to relax and register the fact that your hands are empty—without your calling attention to the fact. (Don't comment, for instance: "Mmm, I'm certainly enjoying this meal with these empty hands of mine." Act normal.)

As you chat, drop your left hand into your lap, and position the creamer in your fist so that its foil top is facing the floor. Pick up a clean fork with your right hand, lean toward

the person across from you, and say, "My eye is bothering me. Do you see anything in it?" As you deliver this attention-focusing statement, pull down the skin of your left cheek with the tines of your fork, revealing the red inner lining of your eye. This alone will skeeze people out.

Don't wait for an answer. Instead, cup your left fist over your left eye so that the hidden creamer's foil top now faces the spectator. Say something like, "Wait . . . I think I can get it—" and slowly thrust the tines of the fork into the foil end of the creamer.

Several things will happen simultaneously: the creamer

container will make a satisfying "pop"; the dairy-product-masquerading-as-eyeball-juice will squirt out of the container, shoot past your fist, and soak the table; and your spectators will jump. If you're lucky, they'll also scream, and on a good night one or two may even faint.

At this point, you have the options of exposing the gaff ("Hey, it was only one of those coffee creamers") or simply dropping the empty container into your lap as you lower your hand to pick up a napkin. (Watch out, though, for potentially embarrassing creamer stains.)

Notes: This trick sounds dangerous, but it's not. Neither Mac nor Mark nor any magician we know has ever seen anyone get hurt by this trick. If you perform it properly, you're piercing the top of the creamer while it's held fast in the center of your fist, not butted up against your eye.

Before trying this trick in public, nab a dozen creamers from a local eatery and practice popping them so you'll get a feel for how much pressure to apply to the foil top during a real performance.

"Eyescream" is not recommended for a first date, unless you've already decided it will be your last, in which case what the heck . . . !

Why This Book Is Good for You

It is of course true that some people will not try the tricks in this book. They feel that they are perhaps too genteel, or too polite, to take center stage and call attention to themselves in a crowd. That's just how I, Mac King, used to feel.

Actually, I've gone through three phases in my off-stage performing persona. When I was younger, I would literally do anything for a laugh. Then, as I began to perform more paid shows, I did less "performing" off stage. The better known I became as a magician and comedian, the fewer shockingly funny and magical things I did in my normal everyday existence. I didn't want folks to think I was always "on." Plus, I think I'm the kind of person who requires a certain amount of public attention, and when that need is sated, I don't go looking for recognition.

I used to think that people liked this shy off-stage demeanor, but I'm not so sure anymore. That's why I've recently shifted over to the third phase of my off-stage life, wherein I will occasionally do something outrageous. Of course, my good friends don't have any desire to see me constantly making a nuisance of myself at the dinner table, but casual acquaintances generally seem to get a genuine kick out of it when I suck a french fry up my nose.

And I predict the same for you. If you're not too over-bearing, and don't make yourself annoying by doing the tricks in this book over and over, then I think you'll find that your friends will like it when you do the occasional gross or funny thing. Really. Mark and I happen to think that it is the mark of a well-rounded person to know a few amazing or funny stunts to show his or her pals.

Also, and maybe you don't want to hear this, or maybe it sounds like preaching to you, but there is something to be learned and gained as a human being from trying these stunts. I mean that seriously. If you take the time to practice a trick, and then work up the nerve to do it for people, you will make some small leap forward in the inner confidence department. Even if you occasionally mess up the trick (which you will, everybody messes up sometimes), you will come out ahead.

Actually, how you handle the sporadic goof-up will tell you a great deal about yourself. If you throw the props across the room and red-facedly berate your audience, chances are good that you need to relax a bit in your everyday life. If you can shrug it off, and make a good-natured joke about your mistake, you'll be much happier. After all, these are only gags. The idea is to create fun—for your friends and for yourself.

Also, you may discover that you have a certain knack for this kind of thing. You'll find that as you perform the gags we've written up here, you'll start to make them seem more "you." Part of the fun of doing tricks and stunts is to put your own imprint on them. Feel free to embellish, edit, or generally enhance any of our head tricks with your own stamp of distinctiveness. The bonus part of this will be that as you make the trick more and more you, and less and less Mac and Mark, the actual secret methodology behind the trick will become more and more hidden, more deeply buried under your personality. And that's what it takes to become a really good magician. So have fun.

The Truth About Cousin Bill

Mac's cousin Bill King drew the original illustrations for the short mock-up he used to try to get this book published. Since those first drawings were done Bill has gone on to become (much to the unqualified bewildered astonishment of everyone in the King family) one of the most sought-after commercial artists in Chicago. As a matter of fact, he has become so successful that instead of the warm forty-ounce bottle of malt liquor he charged for those initial pictures, it cost Mark and Mac an entire case of fine Scotch and forty-eight hours with a hooker to get the brilliant artistic output you see here.

We don't think this book would be the same without cousin Bill's drawings, and we mean that in the nicest way possible.

Mark, Mac, and Bill would like to thank (in an order known only to them): The Levy clan (Stella, Rhoda, Paul, Joyce, and all Mark's other awesome relatives), all the Kings and Sils (Jennifer, Eli, Bettye, John, Elizabeth, Lew, Linda, Caroline, and the rest), Joetta Jackson, Pax and Elwood, Penn and Teller, Lance Burton, Max Maven, David Williamson, Bob Friedhoffer, Brad Stine, Paul Harris, Michael Ammar, David Acer, Brad Ball, Martin Gardner, Rich Marotta, David Pogue, Ron Bauer, Bob Farmer, Gene Matzura, David Regal, Drew Carey, Michael Goudeau, Sid Fleischman, our imaginary friend Binko, Mark Setteducati, Mike Caveney, Glen Strange, Ormond McGill, Tom Mullica, Joel Bauer, Dick Kinney, Larry Becker, Banachek, Mark Jenest, Michael Weber, Charlie and Sherry Frye, Whiskers the Monkey, Gregory Wilson, Nicholas Night, Craig Stone, Eric Mead, Christopher Hart, Brian Campbell, Jon Lovick, Jon Racherbaumer, John Cornelius, John Moehring, John Carney, Jonathon and Charlotte Pendragon, Eric Johnson, Stephen Minch, Bill Goldman, Eugene Burger, Peter Samelson, Michael Chaut, Jamy Ian Swiss, Todd Robbins, Jim Steinmeyer, Ray Hyman, Peter Reveen, Billy McComb, Jay Marshall, Daryl, Tobias Beckwith, Aye Jaye, Pete Studebaker, Looy Simonoff, Bob Escher, Bob Torkova, Joel Hodgson, Stan Allen, Richard Kaufman, Jeff McBride, Roy Silvester, Bill Herz, Mark Kalin and Jinger, Eric Maurin, Bill Voelkner,

Michele Anderson, Stuart Beck, Jeff Hobson, Gary Darwin, Bruce Cervon, Robert Neale, Chris Smith, Al Canal, Alan Shaxon, John Wade, Tom Hamilton, Jack Barnette, Ken Sands, Kerry Pollack, David Groves, Norm Nielson, Fielding West, David Parr, Steve Fearson, Lee Asher, John Thompson, Dan Sylvester, Tom Ogden, Kevin James, Kathleen Murphy, Chris Broughton, Dan Harlan, Mike Bent, Mike Close, Harry Lorayne, Pat Hazel, Jeff Sheridan, Chad Long, Steve "Two Sheds" Sanderson, Karl Weber, Pete Fornatale, and everybody else who helped (or even thought about helping) us get this book published.

MAC KING is the only magician to appear on all five of NBC's highly rated *World's Greatest Magic* TV specials. Mac is the founder of the made-for-TV *Mac King School of Magic*, wherein he has probably started more beginners on the road to magic as a hobby than anyone else ever. As an inventor and magical consultant, his services have been used by Penn and Teller, David Copperfield, and Lance Burton. As an after-dinner corporate entertainer, he has wowed companies around the world with his astounding sleight of hand and irresistible humor. Hailed by many as the premiere comedy magician in the world today, he is currently starring in "The Mac King Comedy Magic Show" at Harrah's Casino and Hotel in Las Vegas, where he resides with his wife and their daughter. Mac has a degree in anthropology and is a swell cook.

In the magic field, **MARK LEVY** is widely known as the co-creator of "Magic for Dummies" which has been hailed as one of the finest books of novice magic ever written. Mark also serves as contributing editor to *Magic Magazine*, was creative director on the New York show "Chamber Magic," and has won awards for his trick-invention skills.

In the business field, Mark has written *Accidental Genius: Revolutionize Your Thinking Through Private Writing*, which was praised by Tom Peters and Ray Bradbury, among others. Mark is also the founder and chairman of Levy Innovation, a firm that helps companies solve problems and create opportunities through original-thinking strategies. Mark lives in New Jersey with his wife Stella.